MH370
Follow the lies to get to the truth

Lachlan Hutchison

Grosvenor House
Publishing Limited

All rights reserved
Copyright © Lachlan Hutchison, 2015

The right of Lachlan Hutchison to be identified as the author of this
work has been asserted by him in accordance with Section 78
of the Copyright, Designs and Patents Act 1988

The book cover picture is copyright to Lachlan Hutchison

This book is published by
Grosvenor House Publishing Ltd
28-30 High Street, Guildford, Surrey, GU1 3EL.
www.grosvenorhousepublishing.co.uk

This book is sold subject to the conditions that it shall not, by way of
trade or otherwise, be lent, resold, hired out or otherwise circulated
without the author's or publisher's prior consent in any form of binding or
cover other than that in which it is published and
without a similar condition including this condition being imposed
on the subsequent purchaser.

A CIP record for this book
is available from the British Library

ISBN 978-1-78148-893-5

The Truth about Malaysian Flight 370?

In 2014 one of the most perplexing aviation mysteries that has ever occurred, has gripped the interest of millions of people from all corners of the planet. A seemingly impossible thing has happened, in this modern world of satellites, radar, radio transmissions and the Internet; a modern passenger airliner, full of people, has taken off, flown for around forty minutes or so, and then by some almost unparalleled sleight of hand, has disappeared without any identifiable trace being left. Despite every piece of modern equipment, from the most advanced countries in the world, being put at the disposal of the searchers, no piece of wreckage or remains of any passenger on board has yet been found. It seems that almost every new piece of evidence simply adds to the confusion and mystery. Amongst all the enormous media coverage, political posturing and scheming, the heartbreaking human loss has all but been forgotten by the wider public. The country of the flights origin was Malaysia, and the Airport was Kuala Lumpur International. The flight was Malaysian Airline MH 370, bound for Beijing in China. This drama played out alongside an ongoing political drama in that country, which I will show heavily influenced the decision making process of the Malaysian Government, and that it was a part of an even greater political drama, played out covertly by two of the world's military super powers.

This book tries to lay out the facts as we know them and quite a few that have not, as yet, been admitted. It will expose the lies that have been told, and that continue to be told. This book will offer a number of possibilities as to what may have happened to Malaysian Flight MH 370 on the night of 8 March and in the following days. It will expose one of the most incredible facts about airlines safety, and how easily flights could still be taken by terrorists; if they so wanted. It will even offer an opinion as to what might happen in the future.

In this book I will explain how I believe that the Malaysian Government lied from the start, and that they also tried to manipulate the disaster for political gain. I will also show that they were completely out their depth in this International drama, and as the pressure mounted on them, they slipped up numerous times and thus, exposed themselves for what they are. It will show that the search for flight MH 370 has been a hoax search from the start, in fact from the morning after the aeroplane went missing. This book will expose that the lives of all on board are regarded as insignificant, as are the sorrows of the bereaved families, to the Politicians at the centre of this mystery.

I will also show that an incredible sleight of hand has happened here, and continues to be happening, it was done perhaps for the correct reason some may argue, and I offer no opinion on that, in that it may very well have averted a war that could have spread throughout the whole of the Middle East and beyond.

These are bold statements, but the facts remain the facts, and there is actually significantly only one explanation that perfectly fits all the things we know; including all the lies we have been told. I will expose these lies and offer substantial evidence to support my assertions.

Timings and distances are the key to deciphering this puzzle; it will expose lies and will expose truths as yet untold, for if a scenario is to be believable it must fit perfectly with the timings we have.

Chapter 1

Timeline

Let us first start with the timeline of events of Flight MH 370.

Saturday 8 March 2014 – Malaysian Airlines Flight MH 370 takes off from Kuala Lumpur International Airport at 41 minutes past midnight (00.41), local Malaysian time, bound for Beijing with 239 souls on board. Flying the plane is a 53-year-old Malaysian man, Captain Zaharie Ahmad Shah, recently separated from his wife of thirty years, father of three, and a proud Grandfather. Captain Shah was a very experienced pilot, and had logged approximately 18,000 hours of flight experience. Captain Shah is a Muslim.

The copilot that night was also a Malaysian man, 27-year-old Fariq Abdul Hamid, who was engaged to be married, and was in fact in the process of planning his wedding. Copilot Hamid was, relative to Captain Shah, inexperienced at his job having logged 2,763 hours on a flight deck; however, this was his very first flight as a fully qualified pilot able to fly a Boeing 777. He had only been in the cockpit of this type of aeroplane on five previous occasions, with this being his first without a training pilot overseeing him. On every other occasion he had flown in the cockpit of a Boeing 777 there had been a total of three flight crew. Copilot Hamid is a Muslim.

There were only two members of the flight crew that night with no navigator, pilot trainers or assessors on board.

The remainder of the Malaysian airline staff are a further ten cabin crew members; all of whom were Malaysian.

People from fourteen different countries were on board as passengers.

There were two hundred and twenty-seven paying passengers of mixed religion, and widespread origins of birth, as you would expect on a flight from one busy international airport to another.

One hundred and fifty-three people of Chinese extraction.

Six Australians.

Two Iranians, who have boarded the plane on false passports, and were said to be heading to Europe to seek political asylum.

Three Americans.

Two Canadians.

Four people from France.

One person from Hong Kong.

Five people from India.

Seven Indonesians.

One Dutch person.

One Russian.

One from Taiwan.

Two Ukrainians.

The aeroplane was a Boeing 777 2H6ER – H6 refers to Malaysian Airlines and denotes type of trim and any other specifications that the Malaysian Airline specified at the time the plane was ordered from Boeing, and ER means Extended Range. The aeroplane was delivered to Malaysian Airlines in May 2002. The maximum range of the craft was 7,941 miles or 12,779 kilometres. The plane had been serviced and safety checked on 23 February 2014, only two weeks before the flight went missing. No issues had been found during the inspections. The only safety red flag being that the aeroplane was damaged in a ground collision in 2012, caused by crashing into another aeroplane whilst taxiing, this accident resulted in an extensively damaged wing tip, this was repaired to the aviation authorities' standard, and the plane had been deemed flight worthy again, and had flown without incident ever since it was repaired.

The flight from Kuala Lumpur to Beijing is approximately five hours and fifty-three minutes long, and this is a vital piece of information. It has been reported that the flight time is in excess of six hours – this is incorrect. The total distance from Kuala Lumpur to Beijing is 2,700 miles, and this again is vital.

The flight distance from Kuala Lumpur to Guangzhu airport in south China is 1,625 miles. The significance of this will be made apparent later.

It was a hot night in Kuala Lumpur and the aeroplane was heavily laden with passengers, their luggage and freight cargo. The passenger manifest was virtually full, the luggage was correctly stowed, and the cargo hold weight limit was made up to its correct maximum limit by crates of mangoes, and some lithium-based batteries. The Lithium batteries weighed about four hundred and forty kilos complete with their packaging, which actually made up half the weight of the batteries total weight. Lithium batteries have in fact brought down a number of flights by causing cargo hold fires, as they can under certain circumstances auto combust, a process that leads to them seemingly bursting into flames for no reason. They must now, by law, be packaged under strict regulation in the correct way, in fireproof containers. It is common practice now for commercial passenger flights to have the holds empty spaces filled with some form of freight to help supplement the running costs of aircraft, so long as the maximum overall weight of the aeroplane does not exceed the manufacturers limit. These limits were correctly respected in the case of flight MH 370 on that night.

The plane took off on time, at 00.41 hours local Malaysian time, and there were no adverse weather conditions, or advisories of such, along the flight path, although there was some low cloud in Kuala Lumpur that night. The flight crew, led by Captain Shah, acted exactly as they should have done during the preflight and take off procedures, and the plane safely climbed to the cruising altitude of 35,000 feet without incident, as per the preflight logged plan. The flight details of every passenger airliner journey are written down in a preflight log by the flight crew, and handed into the air authorities at least one hour before take-off of the flight. This is referred to as the, 'flight plan' and advise all Air Traffic Controllers on the intended route that the aeroplane will be taking, that the flight will be entering their airspace and crossing their borders. It also advises them of other important flight details such as the estimated time the aeroplane will be reaching certain way point radar beacons along that route, course headings, speed, and altitude; this is required to be done as a matter of International Law. The flight plan was filled in and handed in correctly for this journey. The flight plan of all aeroplanes is a vital piece of aviation safety. It has become a vital piece of military information also and I will show later in this book why.

01.07 am – Twenty-six minutes after the flight took off; Flight MH 370 sent its final transponder message. These messages are sent every few moments when the aeroplane is in an area of good radar and transponder coverage, but when an aeroplane is out over large bodies of water the ACARS system stores the information and sends it when it encounters its next radar beacon, usually every half an hour or so. As the aeroplanes cross these radar/transponder markers an antenna receives these messages, this information is then immediately forwarded to the Air Traffic Controllers handling the flight and the information such as, altitude, speed, heading, etc., are accurately updated on the Air Traffic Control computers. The plane is identifiable to the radar towers by its own, unique four-digit code which is attached to the message.

01.19 am – Thirty-eight minutes after the flight took off, as the aeroplane approached the northernmost edge of Malaysian Airspace, whilst out over the South China Sea, just south of the Vietnamese coast, The Copilot Fariq Hamid, is believed to have delivered the last communication from Flight MH 370 to Malaysian Air Traffic Control, signing off from their jurisdiction by saying 'Good night, Malaysian 370,' there was some dispute as to who spoke Pilot or Copilot, however the Federal Bureau of Investigation at Quantico, Virginia in America is believed to have compared the voice that gave the final communication, against known tapes of both the Captain and the Copilot's voices, and proved beyond doubt that it was the Copilot Fariq Hamid who spoke the final words. The final communication was incorrectly given by the Malaysian Government early on in the investigation, as being 'Alright, good night' this is a less formal terminology than the actual message, and whilst it may seem a trivial detail it is actually quite revealing. A pilot would tend to use the formal message that was actually given in this case, as they always state the plane's name – Malaysian 370 – but if a hijacker had taken the plane then you would probably expect to hear the less formal reply, which does not include this information as they would probably be unaware of how communications is handled between Pilots and Air Traffic Controllers, maybe a simple translation fault at the time by the Government Minister, or maybe he had been told the final words, simply forgot and then misreported what he thought they said. It may show a break down in the Malaysian Government information chain, or something more sinister, perhaps he reported correctly and then the information was later changed, we will never know. However the inconsistencies in the Malaysian Governments reporting of simple facts and their self contradictions from the outset left few people with any faith in them or their statements.

This final communication was as Flight MH 370 left Malaysian air space and would soon be entering Vietnamese airspace – the 01.21 am scheduled communication to Vietnamese Air Traffic Control, two minutes after they had signed off from the Malaysian Air Traffic Control, announcing their entry into Vietnamese airspace never came, and in an almost ridiculous turn of events this was missed and went unreported for at least seventeen minutes. However, many believe it was in fact much closer to an hour, or even an hour and forty minutes, as has been reported before the flight was missed. The Vietnamese further compounded their incompetent show, by then reporting they had found flight MH 370 and that it was flying on route to Beijing, over Cambodia. This was completely incorrect, and the inability of the Vietnamese Air Traffic Control to communicate with, locate and then accurately determine the position of Flight MH 370, as was their responsibility, compounded an already confused situation. In this maelstrom of misinformation and incompetence the search for Flight MH 370 was delayed for four to five hours, in fact until it was declared overdue by the Chinese Air Traffic Control the following morning, an unimaginable show of poor ability and the shocking performance from the Vietnamese undoubtedly helped the plane to disappear so effectively.

Critically the planes ACARS transponder, the devise fitted to passenger jets that every few seconds relays the planes position, flight speed and altitude to Air Traffic Controllers through a series of ground antenna, was believed to have been switched off at 01.07am a full twelve minutes before the final communication at 01.19am, although as the aeroplane was out with the reaches of the ACARS radar beacons it is impossible to say this, despite the fact that the Malaysian Government have continually reported it to be the case. This ACARS system is separate from and differs to actual radar as the ACARS system sends these messages out to listening stations, whereas radar sends a signal out itself and relies on picking up the rebounded wave to gather information. Both the ACARS transponder and the aeroplane communications being lost at around the same time suggests they were switched off intentionally after the final communication was made, as opposed to perhaps a simple mechanical or electrical failure, which would probably have affected one system and not the other. This is critical, as it suggests whoever made the final radio communication to the Malaysian Air Traffic Control was perhaps responsible for the diversion of the plane off its pre-flight agreed route, which was to continue from that position north into Vietnamese airspace and to fly on over Cambodia. The fact that the Flight turned west (left) in a deliberate act almost immediately after this communication is also seen by many people as a sign that one or both of the pilots was involved in this deviation from course, or at least signals that they were involved to some extent. It is also an indicator that whoever sent the last communication was familiar with the controls of a Boeing 777 as this would require the ability to re-programme the in-flight navigation computer, and the ability to disable the transponders and communications, which requires fuses to be removed. It is a well known fact that the American FBI are seriously investigating the pilot and the co-pilot from that night to try and ascertain if there was any reason for them to be involved in the flight going missing. The families of both the Captain and Vice-Captain vehemently deny they could be involved in any criminal or terrorist acts. There is also the possibility that the flight crew turned the aeroplane in a westerly direction in response to an emergency, and not in some criminal act.

The shutting off of the communication and ACARS transponder at more or less the same time effectively rendered the aeroplane invisible to Air Traffic Controllers on the ground. The only way they could have been able to track the aeroplane from that point on would have been by civilian ground based radar, but as the aeroplane was out of the range of the relatively weak civilian Air Traffic Control ground radar stations they did not have that as an option. The fact the plane turned off all the systems it had on board that made it visible to Air Traffic Controllers, at the precise point in time that it could not be seen by ground radar is also very significant, the Malaysian ground radar stretches into the South China Sea quite a long way, as does the Vietnamese ground radar but the two systems fall short of each other and do not overlap, this creates an area in the middle of the South China Sea that is a radar black spot, and it was whilst in this black spot that the Flight MH 370 had switched everything off, and this undoubtedly suggests that someone was deliberately trying to hide the plane as they were deviating it from its prescribed course. The fact that whoever was flying the plane chose this precise moment to change direction would also suggest it was someone with knowledge of the ground radar positions and capabilities, and this again would appear to implicate someone from the flight crew, as this radar black spot is widely known about and would have been common knowledge to the pilots, but not perhaps knowledge a non commercial pilot or hijacker would have. This of course may have been a coincidence in timing. I believe, in short, the timing of the Flight MH 370 going missing is critical, and understanding the important timings will play a huge part in unravelling the truth from fiction in this mystery.

Almost immediately after signing off from the Malaysian Air Traffic Control, Malaysian Flight MH 370 then turned west – in fact, its original pre-flight agreed heading was north, so this was a distinctive turn and would probably have been felt by passengers and cabin crew. It also shows an understanding of the flight deck controls and navigation computers. Latterly the Malaysian government would say they believed the flight joystick controls were not used and that the flight computer had been re-programmed, again showing that whoever was in control had an extensive knowledge of the cockpit controls of the Boeing 777 aircraft. However as the transponder and communications with the aeroplane had been severed before this point I have often wondered how the Malaysian Minister of Transportation could tell this, and they have never explained that fact to this day.

02.15 am – One hour and six minutes later, exactly one hour and thirty-four minutes after take-off from Kuala Lumpur International Airport, Malaysian military radar identified MH 370 just north of the Malaysian Island of Penang, flying up the centre of the Andaman Sea not too far from Phuket Island, which has an International sized airport capable of accepting Boeing 777s.

Thai military radar confirms this and plots the plane flying northeast thereafter, out over the Andaman Sea and gives a last contact position very near to Phuket

MH370 — FOLLOW THE LIES TO GET TO THE TRUTH

Island at 02.15 am, local Malaysian time. This means that the aeroplane had been flying for an hour and thirty-four minutes. This is critical. I will later show that the fuel load on the aeroplane allowed for a definitive amount of time in the air, and that once this one hour and thirty-four minutes was removed from that flight time then many of the supposed Government theories as to the position of the aeroplane were unachievable – and in fact untrue.

Once flight MH370 had negotiated northeast and moved almost out of reach of Thai military radar it turned again to the west.

Many weeks after the plane went missing the Malaysian Government released a synopsis of Flight MH 370's known movements and facts. They claim the flight had continued west from this point and had crossed a part of Indonesia up in the very north of the main landmass, known as Banda Ache, which most people will remember from the Boxing Day Tsunami disaster of 2004. Thai military radar has consistently stated from the outset that the plane was moving northeast up the centre of the Andaman Sea. There are slight contradictions between the two sets of military radar but both seem to agree that the final heading was slightly south but mostly west, or west-southwest to give it its correct name, and that will become very revealing later in the book. It is important to state at this point that no radar signature from any landmass or other aeroplane has had flight MH 370 flying south at any stage of the flight.

Saturday 8 March – Flight MH 370 failed to contact the Chinese Air Traffic Control, and they raised the alarm that the flight was missing, and once it failed to land in Beijing it was declared overdue by the Chinese Air Traffic Control. Once a flight is 'declared overdue' all relevant countries in which the overdue aeroplane over-flew or any Air Traffic Control that communicated with the flight must immediately instigate an investigation as to the planes whereabouts. This was the belated start of the search for Flight MH 370, which the Vietnamese had failed to order many hours before.

Saturday 8 March – This led the Vietnamese to establish, ridiculously belatedly, that the flight had never entered their air space, and had not in fact been flying over Cambodia as they had earlier claimed. MH 370 should have entered Vietnamese airspace as stated in the preflight route plan, but did not and had failed to communicate with the Air Traffic Control a viable reason why it was deviating from its pre-flight planned route. Clearly this should have been red flagged earlier, but it was missed. The Malaysian Government on hearing the facts from the Chinese at Beijing Airport and the revised data from the Vietnamese Air Traffic Control declared it an emergency and started the hunt for flight MH 370.

Saturday 8 March – Initial searches were focused on the South China Sea, around the area below where the final voice communication had been received, immediately south of the Vietnamese delta region. Spotter planes were ordered to fly over the area of sea immediately below the position known to have been where the final communication was sent from, to try and identify any wreckage from the aeroplane and to ascertain if there were any survivors, and Malaysia coastal defence ships were deployed to help with this search and possibly recover any survivors or debris. The Malaysian Government persisted with the search in this area up to a week after flight MH 370 disappeared to no avail. This is a fact that Minister Hussein cannot deny, and I will prove later in this book that he knew already that the aeroplane had crossed the Malaysian mainland and had flown out over the area of water known as the Malacca Straits and that he knew there was no chance of any relevant discovery being made in that area.

Sunday 9 March – Malaysian Minister for Transportation Hussein, releases information in a press conference suggesting the aeroplane may have flown over the Malaysian Peninsula, which is an area in the north of the mainland, close to the border region with Thailand. He hints that he may have a signal that showed the plane flying out into the area of water known as the Malacca Straights. Minister Hussein confirms he is expanding the search into the Malacca Straights as well as the South China Sea. Hussein admits there was some confusion surrounding Flight MH 370's movements after the final communication. It is difficult to understand this statement as the Malaysian military clearly had the aeroplane on its radar the whole time.

Monday 10 March – The Malaysian Government early on in the investigation suggests many different possible scenarios for the plane having disappeared from radar and failing to arrive in Beijing. The Boeing 777 has an enviable safety and reliability record and is considered in the aviation industry as being probably one of the safest aeroplanes ever built. Boeing had however, on an inspection of another Boeing 777, discovered it had a potentially disastrous manufacturing flaw, in that it could develop hairline structural cracks on the fuselage near to the radar antenna on the top rear of the plane fuselage. This could under certain circumstances cause a total in-flight catastrophic disintegration of the main fuselage or rapid cabin depressurisation, although it has to be stressed that no Boeing 777 has ever been lost due to this flaw. Boeing had ordered an immediate inspection of all 777s and in fact this aeroplane, Flight MH 370, had undergone its routine service and would have been checked for this only two weeks prior to its flight to Beijing on the 8 March. This potentially catastrophic flaw was mentioned very early by the Malaysians, as perhaps explaining why the plane had so suddenly disappeared. The catastrophic disintegration of the fuselage would leave the pilot with no chance of saving the aeroplane and little chance of being able to call a Mayday as the depressurisation would suck the breath from his body, and the communications would probably be rendered inoperable by the disintegration of the superstructure anyway.

Monday 10 March – The Malaysian government released the fact that there were two Iranian men on board Flight MH 370 who were travelling on false passports, specifically two stolen passports, which had been stolen from two unrelated, white European men, whilst they had been holidaying in Thailand the previous year. The passports had been used by two men of Middle Eastern appearance whilst boarding Flight MH 370. The older of the two Iranian men, a one Delavar Mohammadreza, who was twenty-nine, used his real passport and not one of the stolen passports when he flew into Kuala Lumpur that night from Iran. The other Iranian, who is only believed to be nineteen years old, is named Pouria Mehrdad, and he flew into Kuala Lumpur some days before, he also used his real passport and not his fake one whilst entering the country. He stayed with a friend in Kuala Lumpur whilst there. The Iranian Foreign Affairs Ministry has given some scant details about both men to the investigators, which they said, proved the men were not involved. This did at least confirm they were both Iranian.

To this day no Government has adequately explained their relationship to each other, if any, however it seems an almost incredible coincidence that two Iranian men from Tehran would choose to leave their homeland simultaneously and would subsequently use stolen passports to gain access to the same flight from Kuala Lumpur to China. It has been said that both parties were in fact on their way to Europe and transiting through China in order to claim asylum in Europe for political reasons. All these coincidental points would suggest the two Iranian men knew each other, but no facts establishing this have been offered. Their trip to Europe through China has been suggested as an unlikely route to take in order to seek political asylum – why they never took one of the many European bound direct flights from Kuala Lumpur and thereby reduce their chances of being caught for passport fraud has never been discussed – amazingly. I will look at this in closer detail later in this book.

Interpol concur – stating they are also looking into other suspect passports on board MH 370.

Monday 10 March – Within two days the Malaysian Transport Minister stated that there were no other false passports used on flight MH370.

Monday 10 March – The US Government says no sign of midair explosion on its spy satellite imagery. This being particularly puzzling for onlookers, for if the Americans could say they witnessed no explosion then they must have information as to the flight path the missing plane took once its course was changed or how would they know where to look for an explosion? Unless they were referring to the original logged flight path which was logged as standard with Malaysian Air Traffic Control an hour before take-off, which they would have been able to reference to help find the expected flight path/speed/time positioning by calculation. Thing is, if they were able to look over stored data checking this expected flight path then surely they could have checked what the plane did, once it was established by the Military radar to have turned west over the Malaysian mainland. This they never did. They simply said 'no proof of explosion'.

Monday 10 March – The Malaysian Government issues a statement indicating they believe the Iranian passengers are not involved. They offer as definitive proof of this the fact the younger of the two Iranian men, Pouria Mehrdad's mother, was waiting for him in Frankfurt airport, and had in fact been in touch with the police there. They offered this 'fact' without a thorough investigation into the two mens history, and this is easily proven, as quite simply insufficient time had lapsed since the disappearance of flight MH 370 to mount such an enquiry. These levels of investigation usually take months or many weeks at the least. Let us not forget that when the terrorists attacked the Twin Towers in America the investigation into who they were took months of exhaustive work by the biggest and most powerful agency in the world, specifically the CIA, and the terrorists in that case did little to hide their names or identities. If it took the CIA months whilst dealing with 'friendly' foreign Governments then, there is no way these two could be exonerated in such a short time frame by the Malaysians.

They had not even interviewed the person that Mehrdad had stayed in Kuala Lumpur with at this point. It almost seemed then that the Malaysian Government was determined to convince the world that the two Iranians were not involved in flight MH 370's disappearance, perhaps because they wanted to shift the focus of suspicion onto someone else. Perhaps they had data they hadn't released. What I can say with certainty is that neither of the pilot's homes had as yet been searched and that seemed really odd considering the flight now looked as though it had been deliberately taken as opposed to have crashed, yet the Malaysian Government could exonerate two foreign nationals that had smuggled themselves on board – all seemed very strange to me.

Tuesday 11 March – The Malaysian Government do initial background checks on all passengers and crew and release a statement saying, 'no terrorist activity responsible for flight loss' – critically four hours later America strongly refutes this and releases their own statement saying, 'Any statement suggesting no terrorism involved, definitely not proven yet.' The Americans had, and continue to be, almost silent throughout this entire incident. This being one of the few statements they have made. This conflicting report between the two Governments regarding the possibility of terrorism proves the Malaysians and Americans weren't communicating properly at this time, and if they weren't in proper communication then how could the Malaysians release that statement of no terrorism? Surely in that situation they would simply say, 'We don't know yet.' I will show later that they may in fact have known, and this was one of many verbal slips that the Malaysian Government, who are not used to such intense media pressure, made.

Tuesday 11 March – Initial thoughts of terrorism were soon discounted however as Malaysian and Thai military radar data showed the plane had turned west around the time of the final communication, but this information was slow in being released, so it took a couple of days before the search shifted to the seas west of the Malaysian peninsula. The Malaysian military radar confirmed the plane had crossed the main body of the Malaysian mainland, somewhere near the mountainous region, close to the border with Thailand. It is reported by the Malaysian Government that the aeroplane had altered its altitude dramatically as it turned west, climbing very high initially, up to 45,000 feet and then descending rapidly to very low altitude, even as low as 5,000 feet or lower. Rumours started to abound as many saw this as a possible radar defeating manoeuvre, which opened the possibility that flight MH 370 had in fact been hijacked, as opposed to crashing due to mechanical malfunction or pilot error. The search was extended to the area of water beneath where this last radar sighting had been received; this was in the Malacca Sea, off the west coast of Malaysia.

Many nations were now involved in the search with a huge array of recorded data being sifted through to establish what could have happened. The search continued in both the South China Sea and the Malacca Sea to the west of Malaysia.

Wednesday 12 March – Without any positive leads to go on and no apparent information to follow the Malaysian Government appeared clueless as to the aeroplanes whereabouts and an information-vacuum was created, leaving the families of those on board distraught. Most people, and especially the relatives and loved ones of those that had been on the flight, simply could not believe that a modern airliner full of people could simply vanish without trace. This in fact seemed so incredible that many believed it was impossible and rumours of a Malaysian Government cover up started in earnest.

Thursday 13 March – Information automatically sent to the British Inmarsat satellite from the missing aeroplanes Rolls Royce jet engines to help establish the efficiency and serviceability of the engines was discovered and it showed that Flight MH 370 could have flown on for a further four hours, as the data being sent from the jet engines had continued for this length of time after the communication from the cockpit had ceased. Critically this proved that Flight MH 370 had not crashed into the South China Sea as initially feared was the case. The satellite in question is owned by a private company called Inmarsat plc, which is a telecommunications company. Every 30 minutes in flight

MH 370's Rolls Royce jet engines would attempt to communicate with this satellite to download performance related data. This is a standard procedure that virtually every passenger jet, and in fact commercial jets use, to help dictate service schedules and record the healthiness of the jet engines. These communications allegedly carried on long after all verbal communications with the pilots had ceased. Initially the Inmarsat people said they had communications for a further four hours. This was a truly startling revelation, and many people started to believe that Flight MH 370 could have been taken to a hidden runway where it was being held in a hostage/ransom situation, and hope for the lives of the passengers and crew was renewed. We were led to believe that the aeroplane offered an automatic handshake to the satellite – why then if this is an autonomous or automatic transmission from the jet engines to the satellite did the aeroplane then not send the detailed information to the satellite once the handshake had been done? Surely that would have been sent, as it is what the system is built for. Yet we are being told that there was an automatic handshake, recognised by the satellite and then no further information – I just cannot believe that. It would be interesting to find out from the Inmarsat people how often this has ever happened.

Friday 14 March – The scientists at Inmarsat changed their initial assessment, which was that the plane flew on for four hour to 'at least five hours'. Later that day they revised this to seven hours, and finally, even eight hours after the final communications from the cockpit were made. The aeroplane had less than seven hours of fuel on board at take off and could never have flown for nine and a half hours. Are the Inmarsat people suggesting the aeroplane was in fact then on the ground with the Rolls Royce engines ticking over, or idling?

Friday 14 March – The final partial communication or handshake, as they have been called by the satellite company, from the aeroplanes' Rolls Royce Jet engines to the Inmarsat satellite, at 08.11 hours on Saturday 8 March 8, ended abruptly, according to the Inmarsat people, and was incomplete. Perhaps suggesting the aeroplane was destroyed at this moment.

Saturday 15 March – The Malaysian Government issued a statement saying, 'deliberate action by someone's hand,' had changed the aeroplanes direction and that someone had deliberately shut off its communication and tracker systems. It was disclosed that the missing planes in-flight navigation computer had been either programmed incorrectly whilst on the tarmac in Kuala Lumpur, or had been re-programmed by someone with advanced knowledge of the navigation system whilst the plane was in flight. This then obviously points to some form of hijack perhaps by a member of the flight crew, as they would have the requisite skill set to re-programme the navigation computer and suspicion falls on the pilot and copilot. It could also have been done by some other person with enough training to do this.

Saturday 15 March – Police finally search the pilot and copilots' houses, which utterly incredibly, had been not been done previously. The reason given for this was the Malaysian police force felt it would be inappropriate and upsetting for the missing flight crews' families to

...re a police search whilst their loved ones were still unaccounted for. The searches of their respective homes produces a flight simulator in the pilot Zaharie Shah's house – it is removed for forensic analysis.

Saturday 16 March – Captain Shah is pictured in the media wearing a 'democracy is dead' T-shirt and is strongly linked to a political party that are the direct opposition to the ruling Malaysian Government Party called National Front. The ruling National Front Party has enjoyed unbroken election success since the country gained independence from the British in 1953. Captain Shah was related to Anwar Ibrahim, who was the leader of the opposition party, and was that same day jailed for sexual offences, specifically sodomy. Many Malaysians felt this was a Government conspiracy to 'payback' the opposition leader, as this was the closest election ever contested since the country gained independence. The fact that Captain Shah was such an ardent supporter of Ibrahim and was in fact in court that day before he flew from Kuala Lumpur on the missing flight to watch the guilty verdict, sparked rumours he may have hijacked the plane as a political protest.

Monday 17 March – The scientists from the Inmarsat Company, realising how important it was to try to help the investigation, poured over the data they had received from the missing aeroplane. They determined it feasible that, although it had never been done before, or even attempted before, they could try to roughly plot the route the missing flight took with the data they had. It should be pointed out at this point that the Inmarsat is a communication satellite and not a tracking satellite.

The data they received contained no information as to the position of the aeroplane at the time the data was sent to the satellite, it seemed all they had to go on was signal strength. Despite all these difficulties, the scientists worked over the only data they had, and in what was at the time hailed as a groundbreaking piece of detective work by the British scientists, they were able to determine a general area from which the satellite had received these communications from flight MH 370.

It suggested an enormous possibility of locations, which were displayed to us as a large curve on a world map, stretching from Indonesia down deep into the Southern Ocean in one direction, or in a sweeping corridor from Phuket Island curving up over most of the Far East and into Kazakhstan and even Afghanistan in the other. The signal could potentially have been from over the land of at least ten different countries, as well as the Indian and Southern Oceans. As the data the scientist were working with was not intended for this purpose, then the area the transmissions were received from could not be made more specific, but at least the Malaysian Government would be forced to investigate the circumstances more thoroughly, as it confirmed that the plane had simply not crashed into the South China Sea as initially thought.

Monday 17 March – Utilising the Inmarsat satellite scientists' ground breaking data which had given some indication as to the potential position of that the last communication – or partial handshake – several Countries re-tasked their military satellites to search these areas. Anyone unfamiliar with the process of re-positioning a satellite to look over a specific area should be made aware of the enormity of this task, it is an incredibly complicated and time consuming job, however, this was perhaps the only chance of finding the aeroplane at this stage, as the initial search area encompassed potentially, a quarter of the planet.

Monday 17 March – A few days after their initially assessment was revised up to seven or even eight hours after the final cockpit communication, the scientists at Inmarsat plc seemed to settle on 08.10am local Malaysian time, the following morning after the flight had disappeared, as being the probable last time that Flight MH 370 and the satellite had communicated ... some seven hours after the final communication with Malaysian Air Traffic Control. This was an incredible revelation in the search for the missing flight and opened up a whole new range of explanations as to what could have happened to the aeroplane. The truth is few people noticed how preposterous this timescale was, I personally noticed it straight away, and this was the catalyst for me becoming very interested in the missing flight, and subsequently writing this book. You see, this aeroplane had taken off the previous night with six hours and forty-eight minutes of fuel on board. No more, no less. So how on Earth would it be possible for this flight's jet engines to still be in-flight-communicating with a satellite seven hours and twenty-nine minutes later? The answer is they cannot, and in fact did not, is the correct answer, so why were we getting this false data? I will come back to this later.

Monday 17 March – Mohd Kairul Amri Selamat was a Malaysian private charter jet flight engineer that was on board flight MH 370 and comes under suspicion also. It is felt that because of his extensive knowledge of aeroplanes he would have the requisite skills to at least re-programme the flight navigation computer and maybe even to fly the aeroplane. His name is mentioned and then he is never mentioned again.

Monday 17 March – Industry experts confirm the seat cushions on passenger airliners are virtually unsinkable regardless of impact severity. These are in fact not mechanically fixed to the aeroplane seats and detach readily when submersed in water. They are designed specifically in this way in case of a crash in water so they might act as a rudimentary floatation device for survivors.

Tuesday 18 March – The search parameters were narrowed significantly by the Inmarsat Company scientists' late night hard work, and their on-going detective work was helping them reduce the initial search areas. However the area was still incredibly vast. It was not lost on anyone that the areas of land that the Inmarsat scientists believed that Flight MH 370 might have come down on, reached the Jihadists strongholds of Northern Pakistan, Afghanistan and Turkmenistan. Most observers at that point believing it was a real possibility that the plane had been hijacked by Islamic extremists and flown to a secret airbase in one of these countries, where it would be used at a later date as a human guided missile to attack Western targets, just as the Jihadists had done on September the Eleventh attacks on Manhattan Island years before.

Wednesday 19 March – A few more days into the investigation the scientists from Inmarsat stated they believed that the flight 'probably' went south, towards the Southern Ocean. I can remember at the time seeming incredulous about this revelation as there was absolutely nothing there but open Ocean, and many people – especially the families of those on board – believed that this made no sense at all. Why hijack a plane to fly it all the way down there for hours with the seemingly pointless intention of allowing it to crash into the sea? It was still believed, in fact hoped, that the flight had been hijacked and the plane landed safely somewhere with everyone on board still alive. The relatives of those on board wanted to believe this scenario, perhaps as this scenario was the one that could afford their loved ones some possible hope of life.

Wednesday 19 March – Information is released from the Thai Military, stating that radar shows the flight believed to have been flown as low as 5,000 feet and as high as 45,000 feet, potentially to avoid radar detection, although some point to the parabolic flight characteristics as being typical of a captain trying to use thrust, G force and gravity as a counter cockpit attack manoeuvre. This was the procedure adopted by most airlines and Governments post 11 September 11 attacks on the USA, whereby a pilot detecting an attempted flight deck storming would immediately go to full power from all engines and basically stand the aeroplane on its tale in as steep a vertical climb as possible. This would serve a few purposes, primarily to allow the copilot a few seconds opportunity to subdue the assailants by 'fighting downhill' and use gravity and thrust to help him to propel the would be aggressor backwards away from the cockpit. At this point he and the flight attendants would enlist the help of the passengers to subdue the assailants by weight of numbers. Handcuffs are in fact present on all flights nowadays in case of this, to manacle would be attackers to their seat if necessary.

Thursday 20 March – Further groundbreaking analysis by the British scientists of the Inmarsat satellite data proved the aeroplane was, according to them, 'definitely' on the southern portion of the potential flight routes into the Southern Hemisphere – taking it away from land where many had hoped, or thought the aeroplane had been hijacked to, and into the Southern Oceans, the Scientists helped to pinpoint an area still ridiculously deep into the Southern Ocean.

Thursday 20 March – Rough calculations were made as to possible speed and duration of flight and an area deep in the Southern Ocean was identified as a possible final destination for the flight. Not one person said so at the time, but as a point of fact, if Flight MH 370 had taken off from Kuala Lumpur that night and flown directly to the Southern Ocean without its more than one hour detour north, it would not have had enough fuel to reach the position that the search parties were sent to initially. It simply did not have the fuel on board, and remember it had flown north and then northwest for more than an hour and a half before it could even have turned south, more lies I am afraid. As a point of fact it is 2,700 miles from Kuala Lumpur to Beijing. It is 2,600 miles from Kuala Lumpur to Perth Australia, however the initial search area was more than 500 miles south of that.

Remember the flight flew north for at least an hour and thirty-four minutes first. This is confirmed by the Thai military radar. So that would reduce the actual journey south, by very close to two hours and forty minutes, if we allow for the fact that the aeroplane was flying west for a part of its journey and not north and thus not actually flying any further from the Southern Ocean. Flight MH 370 took off with six hours forty-eight minutes of fuel on board – fact – so if we subtract the one hour thirty-four minutes from the total fuel time of six hours and forty-eight minutes that leaves five hours fourteen minutes total flying time from the final radar contact made by the Thai military at 02.15am that puts the plane in the Andaman Sea. No matter who you are, the mathematics are very simple. The plane flies at a cruising speed of roughly five hundred and fifty miles per hour. Multiply that by the fuel/time left on board and you get the maximum range that the plane can fly before it crashes into the ocean. The maximum distance the flight could have covered from the last confirmed contact in the Andaman Sea is two thousand eight hundred and eighty-seven miles, and that is if the aeroplane was flying at its optimum height of 35,000 feet and optimum air-speed, which Thai radar suggests it was not, the military radar has the aeroplane at 5,000 feet, and an aeroplane at that height can use a third more fuel per hour and that would mean a third less distance.

Fuel consumption would also be greatly affected by the aeroplane having to re-climb up to 35,000 feet from the agreed altitude of 5,000 feet it was at just off of Phuket, if it did at all, to make the optimum flight altitude as regards economy of fuel. So either way, if it stayed low or climbed high to reach the optimum cruising altitude and speed, it would have used an enormous portion of its fuel, and the two thousand eight hundred mile range would have been utterly impossible. The initial search in the Southern Ocean was nearly three thousand seven hundred miles from the last confirmed contact. They were searching eight hundred miles too far south and that is if the aeroplane had been at a constant 35,000 feet since it took off from Kuala Lumpur, which we know it was not.

If you revise the calculation and take into account the known altitude variations of the flight that night, I think the initial search was closer to fifteen hundred miles too far south! Is this a joke? Are the people organising this search unable to do simple mathematics? Or are they hiding something? Once this ridiculous search area was determined then the Australian Government became heavily involved in the search, as they were the nearest significant landmass to the estimated crash site with sufficient resources to mount this search. A wide array of equipment was directed to the Southern Ocean to help the search; spotter planes and ships and a specialised towed 'pinger' locator from the United States. A highly specialised deep-sea submarine drone, called the Bluefin-21 Autonomous Drone System, was also sent to the Australians. This piece of equipment can dive very deep, up to four thousand five hundred meters and once there it can use its highly sensitive, side scan sonar to take 3D images of the seabed. This would be vital in the very deep waters they had been sent to search. It would be pre-programmed to follow an overlapping grid pattern over a designated area. It is capable of covering huge areas of the seabed in a short space of time. Once these 3D images have been downloaded from the submarine drone, which takes place after it has re-surfaced, they would be checked over to see if any sign of the wreckage is lying on the seabed. A nuclear submarine was redeployed to the search area by the United Kingdom, although what exact roll it was expected to play was never divulged, and one would think its usefulness would be limited. The towed 'pinger' locator is used to find the black box cockpit data recorder, and the cockpit voice recorder, as they both emit a 'ping' on a designated frequency, which the pinger locator can identify. The system is designed to be towed behind a ship on a very long steel cable, and can reach very deep depths of up to two thousand five hundred meters. These three different and completely separate systems were all part of a multi-national attempt to provide the search teams with all the equipment they might need to help find the crashed aeroplane. Both of the black boxes have similar pingers, which are activated on contact with water, and crucially have a four week battery life, after which they go silent and would then prove virtually impossible to find, and this was one of the main reasons there was so much effort being put into finding them as early as possible. Or so we were constantly told. I believe this is untrue. I believe that every attempt to stall this investigation was being made, and had been made consistently from the start, specifically to run the batteries on the black boxes down. Later in this book I will show the proof of this.

Thursday 20 March – Many nations now turned to their expensive, and often highly classified, military spy satellites, in order to scan the newly designated target area in the Southern Ocean, hundreds of miles South of

Australia. These satellites have a wide array of sensitive systems on board that can use many different ways of detecting potential aircraft debris from space, to try to find the missing aeroplane. Satellite imagery from a French military satellite, initially showed real promise and looked to have identified a large white piece of wreckage which we were told was up to fifty metres in length and resembled the tail section of a passenger airliner. They offered the evidence to the search teams and pointed them to an exact position some 1,500 miles southeast of Australia; spotter planes and surface ships were dispatched to the location by the Australians, but despite many days of arduous flying and often in hazardous conditions, they were, eventually, unable to locate any debris consistent with the images given. At one point the searching teams were stood down from the search as the Southern Ocean location pinpointed by the French provided weather conditions simply too hazardous for either planes or shipping to venture in to.

Great frustration was felt at this time by the families of those on board as to the lack of progress, obviously their hope being for some kind of miracle. I will later show that this might have been a false trail set by the Malaysian and American Governments to have every satellite involved in the hunt for Malaysian Flight MH 370 looking in the wrong place, in fact, in a place that the flight could never have reached. This may have been important to them, as a satellite looking in the correct place might have ruined their sleight of hand trick.

Thursday 20 March – Almost two weeks after the flight had vanished Thai satellite imagery offered a different location five hundred miles further north from the initial search site, where potential crash debris might be found, again, and despite this search zone being north of the 'Roaring Forties' extreme low cloud and precipitation, allied to high winds and corresponding high seas forced a further cancelation of the searches. The planes being grounded on the tarmac in Australia, and the ships were removed to an area further north to ride out the storm. The following day the search resumed still under questionable weather conditions, and whilst being hindered by low cloud and reduced visibility the search teams were unable to find any trace of the missing aeroplane.

Monday 24 March – Malaysian Prime Minister Najib Razak, whom had been conspicuous by his silence to this point, tells the world in a press conference in Kuala Lumpur that having consulted world aviation experts they had established beyond any reasonable doubt that the missing flight, Malaysian Air MH 370 had crashed in the Southern Indian Ocean and that the full complement of passengers and crew had perished there, without any hope of any survivors. Razak said this without naming one expert that they had consulted, or having a single shred of hard evidence to show in support of this statement, he simply dismissed the passengers and crew as dead, in what for me was a very unsympathetic and almost callous speech, critically he states the Indian Ocean not Southern Ocean, which are two distinctly different bodies of water. All the while the initial searches were continuing in the Southern Ocean, southwest of Australia.

Friday 28 March – Australian, Chinese, and Malaysian Government, backed by American experts suggest heavily that although they will continue to try for as long as is humanly acceptable, they may never find the plane; or the black boxes or the answers to this mystery. They continue to cite the fact that this is such an inhospitable part of the planet, constantly beset by high seas and even higher winds, and that the water there is so deep, that this may eventually prove to be a bridge too far.

Friday 5 April – Chinese research vessel the *Haixun 01* detects pings consistent with those given off by black box recorders with acoustic microphones. This was in an area of water thought to be where Flight MH 370 had crashed, much further north than the initial search area. The water depth in that area is a minimum of 4,500 metres and bottoms out at 8,000 metres plus. We were previously told that the acoustic ping given off by the black boxes could be heard at a maximum of 2,000 metres from *the black box in water. No one mentioned this in regard to this acoustic signature.*

Saturday 16 April – The Australians also pick up an acoustic ping on the correct frequency. This is also in extremely deep water and is picked up twelve hours after the Chinese had detected their acoustic ping signal. This was in an area of water three hundred nautical miles from where the Chinese had had their success. Again ... no one mentioned this obvious anomaly. It is ridiculous to suggest that the two black boxes were separated by this distance.

Wednesday 23 April – Debris consistent with a crashed aeroplane and showing colours of the Malaysian Airline are reported to have washed up on a beach on the southwest of Australia. It is later collected and deemed not to be from the missing flight.

Friday 25 April – Australian Prime Minister announces that the possibilities of finding any floating debris from the missing flight are now virtually non-existent, as any debris that had survived the impact of the aeroplane crash and remained on the surface would have become waterlogged due to the extended passage of time, and would have now sunk. He further stated that the underwater search by the American submarine drone was nearing completion and that no trace had as yet been found. The Australian Prime Minister conceding that it might in fact prove impossible to ever find any trace of the missing flight. Under his orders the aerial/visual search by aeroplanes and spotter personnel would be ended and the search would still carry on with the sub-surface equipment and surface fleet.

Wednesday 30 April – Australian company Geo-Resonance that use ex-military satellites that were commissioned to find nuclear submarines and nuclear warheads during the cold war, and that is now used to search for traces of valuable minerals, claim to have found something in the Bay of Bengal. This is three thousand miles from the Southern Ocean search area being prosecuted by the Australian search contingent. The GeoResonance scientists believe they have detected the chemical signatures of metals consistently found in Boeing Aircraft, specifically Aluminium, Copper, Titanium and intriguingly jet fuel residue.

Wednesday 30 April – An American civilian with a private recreational flying licence claims to have found the missing flight in the Gulf of Thailand; close to the area over which the flight initially vanished. The image he found reportedly shows an intact aeroplane fully submerged in shallow water.

Friday 2 May – The Malaysian Government releases all the facts it knows to date. This includes all the military radar data and communications from Air Traffic Controllers and the Conversations heard from the pilots. Some of this completely contradicts their earlier statements.

Monday 5 May – The Malaysian Police confirm the arrest of eleven men in Kuala Lumpur on suspected terrorism charges, linked to Flight MH 370. It is revealed that a UK male with known international connections to terrorism had built a shoe bomb and had it delivered to the leader of a new terrorist group based in Malaysia. It was to be used to blow open the security door on a passenger liner. The terror group was said to have links to Al Qaeda, and were acting under instruction from one of the world's most hunted terrorists, Khaled Shaik Mohammed.

Chapter 2

So what happened to Malaysian Air Flight MH 370 on that fateful night?

Let me first state that, in no way, am I apportioning blame to any party in this book. I will provide factual evidence, supposition and use detective intuition, to put forward scenarios that may or may not have happened. I will honestly debate each possible scenario and put the pros and cons for each side as I see them. Ultimately the reader must make his own decisions as to possible guilt or innocence of anyone or any parties.

There are a number of possible scenarios that have been put forward that could explain the disappearance of flight MH 370 and I will outline them first ... most have numerous flaws, and some are down-right ridiculous ... there is however, more than one scenario that seem to fit all the facts and, one in particular, never mentioned before that may hold the answer.

Scenario 1. Catastrophic In-flight Disintegration.

Initially touted by the Malaysian Government, on the morning after they were told by the Chinese the flight had gone missing, as the most likely cause of the flight going down over the South China Sea. Subsequent revelations from radar, and engine telemetry data picked up by satellites communicating with the aeroplane's Rolls Royce jet engines has made this seem the least likely of all scenarios. The transponders being switched off, then the communications also being switched off and the altering of the flight plan completely discredit this. Along with the fact there is no debris.

Scenario 2. In-flight fire.

This should not be discounted and is a very real possibility, in fact more than one commercial pilot and many captains believe this to be the real reason the flight went missing. That may well be because, through a sense of brotherhood and kinship with their fellow pilot, it is a scenario that they believe paints the pilots in a positive light and actually portrays them as heroes. Despite a near perfect flight record, and with only recent accidents denting this impeccable record, the Boeing 777 does have a couple of recognised faults – An Egypt Air Boeing 777 was declared a complete write off due to a cockpit fire whilst still on the tarmac, and full of passengers, at Cairo airport three years prior to Flight MH 370 going missing.

The plane that day developed an electrical fire under the right hand side cockpit window. The fire took hold quickly and aggressively – very aggressively in fact – and despite the immediate attempts by the pilot to extinguish the fire using the fire extinguisher provided and the speedy attendance of the Airport fire crews, the fire quickly got out of hand and fire crews took an hour to bring the fire under control. The result of the fire was a large hole burnt completely through the fuselage beside the captain's seat and an utterly destroyed cockpit, all of which lead to a destroyed aeroplane. Thankfully that incident occurred on the ground and shortly before take-off, as the result would have clearly been catastrophic for everyone on board if it had happened after take-off. The flight attendants that day acted brilliantly and the plane was successfully evacuated without loss of life or serious injury. The fire was subsequently proved, under investigation by the Air Authority to have started near to the rubber tubing coming from the co-pilots oxygen mask. This is the pressurised replacement pilots use under emergency conditions whilst at altitude. The pressurised oxygen fed the flames and expanded the fire very quickly and thus rendered the fire fighting capabilities of the crew utterly inadequate.

There was a FIA directive that these rubber tubes should be replaced immediately. It has never been established whether the rubber hoses on Flight MH 370 had ever been replaced. This does, however, show a fire is at least possible, and given the almost explosive spreading of the flames, witnessed in the Egypt Air flight, could explain why no Mayday was sent as the flight crew would be pitched instantly into a battle of life and death with the fire. We can also deduce that the fire fighting equipment on board would be inadequate to defeat this fire, or even suppress it for any length of time. This would rapidly develop into a fire that would either kill the pilots due to smoke inhalation and heat or at very least drive them out of the cockpit. The extremely aggressive nature of this particular fire would definitely have destroyed the aeroplane in a reasonably short space of time. It is unconceivable that the plane could have flown if it was as extensively damaged as the Egypt Air 777.

However, another reason for a less aggressive fire in the cockpit could be an overheated front tyre on the landing gear. This has happened before and is a known reason for aeroplane fires. It could possibly have smouldered for a while in the front landing gear storage bay, which is located slightly behind the cockpit, having been overheated on take-off. As I say this has happened before and there are numerous precedents for this. Remember it was a hot night, hot tarmac and a very heavily laden aircraft running at near maximum weight. If the wrong conditions existed in the storage bay, it could have smouldered in there for a considerable period of time and then eventually, caught alight or even burst into flames aggressively. The fire would be in a bad area in the front landing gear storage bay, close to the forward engineering room, which is just forward of this position and contains a huge amount of flammable wiring looms. If the fire spread into these wiring looms they would burn readily giving off thick black acrid smoke.

This is the area directly below the cockpit and would cause the cabin to rapidly fill with smoke and after a relatively short time, with flame also. Whilst it may sound unlikely it has happened before, and the timing of the fire, almost an hour after take-off was similar then and due to the difficulty in accessing the area the fire was seated in, proved impossible to extinguish. The aeroplane crashed with the loss of all on board. All modern passenger aeroplanes, such as this, have fire detection systems on board in cargo holds and engineering rooms, but are only legally required to provide fire suppression systems in the cargo hold areas, not the landing gear storage bay, or the forward engineering compartment. Typically these fire suppression systems use Halon, which is in a pressurised canister, to firstly defeat the fire, and then by maintaining high levels of Halon in the compartment, suppress the fire for a minimum of an hour. The low levels of oxygen at high altitude makes it difficult for things to combust in the cargo area and landing gear storage bay. Something catching fire as the plane takes off however, would have enough oxygen to combust as there is obviously more oxygen nearer ground level. Fires have been known to start during the take off period of the flight and then die back and smoulder for a long time or even extinguish due to the thin air at altitude.

Held in the cargo hold on Flight MH 370 were Lithium batteries. There were 220 kilograms of batteries correctly packaged in fire-proof boxes, making the total weight of the batteries and packaging up to 440 kilograms. Lithium batteries are significant in that they are very dangerous if they are incorrectly packaged or damaged. They can auto combust; or in layman's terms burst into flame. They have been responsible for bringing down aircraft before and must now be packaged in fire-proof boxes as a result. When they do auto combust the Lithium batteries prove very difficult to extinguish and even Halon is unable to extinguish such a fire.

As with any complex wiring system – the Boeing 777 has four miles of cable in it to manage all the various systems on board – there will always be a chance of an electrical short-circuit and possible fire. The electrical systems are very well isolated and protected by circuit breakers; however it has been shown that this is no guarantee of absolute protection from the risk of fire.

So if we accept that a fire could have started on board through one of these situations then this is how this scenario might have happened.

A fire started somewhere in the forward area of the aeroplane and went undetected by the smoke alarms. It may well be that it did indeed start in the forward landing gear storage bay where there are no smoke detectors or fire suppressors. The fire spread slowly due to lack of oxygen at high altitude but had enough of a seat to burn on. The pilot and copilot were still unaware they had a fire on board. The fire happened to melt the electric cables that supply the ACARS transponder with power, and after a short circuit it was silently disabled. The fire continued to burn and reached the cabling that supplied the communications control. The copilot meanwhile, still unaware that there was a fire, did the routine hand off to the Malaysian Air Traffic Control as they left Malaysian Air Space. Very shortly after that the fire fatally damaged the communications and the plane was left unable to communicate. Either this or the fire spread so rapidly that the captain and copilot were so consumed with the immediate need to fire fight they had no time to raise the Mayday alarm. Either way this could explain how the ACARS and then communications were rendered inoperable. All flight crew, and in fact, all crew, are aware of the dangers of a fire onboard whilst in the air. The golden rule, according to the NTSC is that an aeroplane has twelve minutes to land once a fire has started or the chances of survival are greatly reduced. For this reason, all airline crews undergo fire training on a regular basis. Of course the timing of the event on board might cause some to disbelieve this scenario, but they do happen.

With a sudden and serious fire in and under the cockpit area all hands would be brought to bear immediately to fight the fire. The sub floor area on a Boeing 777 is accessed from the forward galley, and whilst one of the pilots would undoubtedly be fighting the fire in the cockpit, then the other would need to get the hatch open and climb down the ladder to fight the fire down below. In this instance he would rush down and attack the fire immediately, I think, as he would know through his training that seconds are vital, when it comes to attacking a fire. Crucially he may have underestimated the severity of fire, or in fact just never stopped to put on the replacement air mask with cylinder attached, due to knowing he needed to attack this fire immediately. He may have perished soon after climbing down due to smoke inhalation, perhaps even, still fighting the fire. The other cabin crew now wearing their replacement air masks would follow him down and using the Halon and Carbon Dioxide extinguishers manage to get the fire out. The captain who had been also heroic in his attempt to fight the fire had also perished, succumbing to the smoke and heat. This may sound far-fetched but in fact both pilots would know better than anyone if they did not extinguish the fire they would be sure to die anyway, so may well have just kept fighting in desperation. This has also been done before. The navigation system may have also been damaged or destroyed. Truth is it would not make any difference. If it was destroyed then whoever decided to jump in the pilot's seat would needed to have acted quickly. In a smoke filled cockpit they would realise they were descending and would need to pull back on the flight controls, and anyone would know to do that. They may have even still had their replacement air mask on, which commonly suffer from misting, and in a hot cockpit whilst fighting fire it would definitely have done so. They might have climbed the aeroplane further than they realised, or in fact may have even been unable to see through their mask. This might explain the rapid climbing and descending of the flight, as it has been shown to have done after the final communication. However this climb would, I fear, have had disastrous affects also. There are smoke detectors in the passenger areas on all passenger aircraft and if they sense a fire they immediately deploy the drop down masks we are all familiar with from the in-flight safety brief. These drop-down masks do not as you would think have an endless supply of tank fed air. In fact they are fed by a small air generator that is driven by the jet exhaust. It has about ten minutes of air in it, no more. The people on board would have automatically put these on. Remember it was a full flight and ten minutes of air is all they could deliver to this many people. With the flight now being flown by a complete novice, and someone with no flight experience of flying in daytime let alone at night, they would obviously be afraid, terrified even, and in a smoke filled cabin with probably no lights and reduced visibility due to the air mask they continued to climb. Instinct I think in this situation would drive just about everyone to do the same. You would undoubtedly be afraid of crashing into the ground so would be determined in your fear for that not to happen.

The nightmare is that the fire may have in fact caused a hole in the airtight fuselage, as happened in the Egypt Air flight, and this would be catastrophic for the passengers. In fact the fire causing a hole in the fuselage could actually explain why the flight did not immediately crash. The rapid depressurisation of the aeroplane might have extinguished the fire, or at least helped the crew fighting it, and if both pilots were fighting the fire without having put on a replacement air crew mask, and had not as yet succumbed to the fire, they would have died of asphyxiation at that altitude in a very short period of time anyway. The air generator in fact does not work above 40,000 feet anyway, but as it had already surpassed the ten minutes of air if could deliver this was immaterial. At those altitudes of 45,000 feet the passengers would have been killed by asphyxiation in a matter of a few seconds; thirty to sixty at most. The air pressure at that altitude is so low the air is utterly sucked from your lungs. So the cabin crew alone would have survived the initial emergency, with both Pilots either dying because of smoke inhalation/heat or asphyxiation, as they alone would have been wearing their pressurised cylinder replacement air.

The passengers would have simply gone to sleep and very little could have been done to prevent it, and this might have even gone unnoticed by the crew who would also be struggling to see through the misty glass on their masks. It may well be that the cabin crew perished as well at that point, as they would have had their masks on to fight the fire, and once it was defeated, depending on how long it took, would have depleted their cylinders. Any attempt by them to use the Passengers drop-down mask would have proved futile, and death would have been very quick. The fact the plane was at 45,000 feet for twenty-two minutes is perhaps indicative off this also. The cabin steward now flying the plane would have put on the captains replacement air mask once the one they had on had emptied. This would provide whoever was now flying the aeroplane at least twenty minutes of air, and the copilots air supply would have been untouched so they could effectively have forty plus minutes or more. I am afraid to say that I think by the time first canister of the new pilots air was emptied, which would have happened after about twenty minutes or so. The fact was the case with the flight, that despite the heroic efforts of the captain and copilot and the entire cabin crew the person flying the plane may have been the only person left aboard still alive and they may have not even known that at that point. As they would at this point need to change over masks to put on the copilots they may then have noticed the altimeter was at 45,000 feet, and as a flight attendant would know they were too high. They would also know to descend to 12,000 feet as it is part of their training to know this, and this again is what the aeroplane did.

If a fire did occur, and this scenario is in fact what happened, then let us try to explain the route and altitude variations that the flight took that night and see if there is some way to explain this. The member of the cabin crew now flying the plane, whoever it was, would now face an incredibly difficult set of problems. The first problem is that they cannot fly any higher than

12,000 feet as they would have to use the replacement air again and I think I can say with some certainty that they would not want to do that again. They would probably be starting to realise that they were alone, and that all was not well with their work colleagues and passengers, as there was no one coming in to see them. They could not leave the cockpit to find out what was happening as the navigation computer also known as the auto pilot, was destroyed, and they needed to stay where they were to fly the plane. During the initial emergency and subsequent fire fighting, followed by having to fly the aeroplane the new pilot would have become unbelievably disoriented, I think we can say that would be normal. The cabin crewmember would have very little idea where they were in relation to any land or sea below them, as it is not important for them to keep up to date with flight position during the course of their work as stewards. They would have no communications with which to call for help as these were destroyed in the fire. It was nighttime they were totally out of their comfort zone and hopelessly lost. Even working out the time that had elapsed may have proved a challenge. And the only means of navigating would be a compass and their eyesight. The initial turn west may have been unintentional or may have been initiated by the captain or copilot at the very start of the emergency, either way I am sure this would be hugely disorienting for someone with no flight experience.

They would know they were supposed to be flying north and may have not even known they had passed over the Malaysian mainland. So they decided to turn back north, as they would think they were still over the South China Sea and not in fact over another body of water, the Malacca Straights, with a view to attempting to land at Ho Chi Minh City Airport in Vietnam or Phnom Penn Airport in Cambodia.

Sadly by the time they turned north they were hopelessly out of position. So whoever was flying then decided to drop down below the cloud cover, in fact down to 5,000 feet as the Thai radar has shown us, and attempts to get some form of visual confirmation, or some visual reference of a landmark known to them, in order to get their bearings as to their location. This was also done by the aeroplane, and the person flying dropping down to desperately try and catch site of anything so that they could to try and save their own life, has perhaps been wrongly interpreted as someone trying to fly low to avoid radar. The turn north and the dropping down lower to see if they could find somewhere to land the plane however was in fact a horrendously unlucky decision, just another in a night of incredible bad luck, as the aeroplane flew right up the middle of the Andaman Sea and continued north as we have been told by the Thai Military. The new pilot would now be becoming frantic, as the land they expected to see in front of them never appeared. Desperation would sink in and they would compound their bad luck with understandably poor decision making whilst under enormous stress. If they believed they were still in the South China Sea they would not turn east as they would know there is no land there, so eventually they decided to turn west again in the hope of finding land in that direction.

After a prolonged period of flying west again and with no sign of any land, the, by now panicking, crew member decided to turn south and would stay on that course perhaps zig-zagging as they went in desperation. All the while taking the plane further away from safety, until at some point in the early hours of the morning the plane ran out of fuel and crashed into the sea, leaving the entire compliment of crew dead. The cabin crew-member, who has to be applauded for their resilience and determination throughout this series of catastrophic events, may have even attempted to land the aeroplane in the water, as they would undoubtedly have noticed the fuel reserves running low, in a final attempt at saving their own life. This is a highly skilled manoeuvre and definitely beyond the capabilities of someone so inexperienced. The plane would almost certainly have broken up on contact with the water and taken its final victim in the process.

Even if one of the pilots survived the initial fire this scenario is still a possibility, especially if it was the copilot as he was just qualified and relatively inexperienced. Every qualified pilot I have spoken to about this case has mentioned the extremely disorienting task of flying an aeroplane at night, over water. The copilot may have even been seriously injured in the fire as well, to compound his problems. Don't think it is an unusual thing for a pilot to get lost in these circumstances, as it is very common. President J F Kennedy's son, himself a relatively inexperienced pilot died at the controls of his own aircraft whilst flying to Martha's Vineyard in America at night, an area he knew well, but he became disoriented while over the water, which caused him to crash, and his wife and sister-in-law perished that night along with him. This is not the only case of this happening. The turn west, I have been told, is the route that most pilots would have taken in an emergency for the simple reasons that it would allow them to turn back over land almost immediately, this is always preferable to being over water in an emergency, and this would give him the opportunity of landing at either Phuket International Airport, or Penang Island Airport, and the island of Penang has its airport in the north so he could land without circling, and do a very simple fly in, which would be the preferred way.

This would also be advantageous if they were concerned about the engines failing and leaving them without power so that they would have to glide in to the runway, and they would have only a very short part of the flight over the little water between the Malaysian mainland and the Island itself, which is a few short kilometres, this would explain the sudden change of direction and it could explain the rapid climb to 45,000 feet, so he had sufficient height in case he had to glide in if his engines failed, or it may be that the pilot made the mistake of over climbing to too high an altitude in an attempt to help defeat the fire. Now once he crossed the Malaysian peninsula to reach the west coast, instead of heading south, to Penang Island, he turns north, as proved by the Thai military radar. This may be an indication that he had chosen the Thai Island of Phuket as his emergency runway, but it may be that with his limited navigational equipment and the fact that this was his very first flight as a fully qualified pilot he became as disoriented as the cabin steward I discussed earlier in this possible scenario, and then suffered the same fate.

There is no doubt that the scenario where the cabin steward flying the plane and getting lost is the one that would seem the more likely of the two possible cases here. Most people would feel the copilot would have the necessary skills to find an airport and land the plane, but a relatively inexperienced pilot like this, at such an early time in his flying career in a strange aeroplane, and under such duress, and perhaps seriously injured, at night, is capable of similar mistakes and for sure this has happened before. This scenario as I said before is the one most pilots believe and there is no doubt it covers most of the points that we know as fact. It does not however explain why no wreckage has ever been found.

Scenario 3. Rapid Cabin Depressurisation.

The Boeing Company have identified a potential inherent structural flaw in the Boeing 777. There is a possibility, over a significant period of time, that the fuselage can develop a crack near to the radar mounting point, on top of the aircraft, towards the rear of the passenger compartment. This can in some circumstances lead to a rapid depressurisation of the passenger compartment and in an extreme case could lead to a catastrophic complete structural failure of the aeroplane; this has been stated by the FAA and Boeing.

For this scenario to work, once again the flight would have had to take off and climb to cruising altitude without incident. Shortly after the copilot handed off verbally to the Malaysian Air Traffic Control, a known fault in the Boeing 777 occurred, specifically a large crack close to the radar mounting on the top of the plane to the rear of the passenger compartment. The hole is sufficient to cause an instantaneous cabin depressurisation, affecting both the cockpit and passenger areas. The cockpit and cabin areas are obviously separated by the cockpit security door, which have special blow out panels in them, so that in the event of a rapid decompression of the passenger area the cockpit area is equally affected by depressurisation, primarily so that the pilots are aware that a decompression event has occurred, and also in case one of them tried to open the door of a pressurised cockpit into a depressurised cabin, as he would be violently sucked out of the cockpit by the outrush of air from the cockpit.

Suddenly and without warning whilst one of the pilots is out of his seat, perhaps using the toilet facilities, this rapid decompression takes place. In the cockpit the master alarm sounds and the cabin pressure warning light flashes red. The aeroplane has developed an enormous gaping hole six feet (1,800 mm) wide by ten feet (3,000 mm) long where the roof of the plane has opened up and is now open to the elements, the roof of the plane is bent back over to look like an enormous car spoiler lying on the top of the aeroplane, this instant change in the aeroplane's aerodynamic performance simultaneously pitches the aeroplane's nose down and it starts to descent rapidly. The huge tear has ripped cabling from it cable stays and bare end of cable spark as they short-circuit. This short-circuiting causes a power surge that lifts a series of breakers in the cockpit wiring control board, amongst which are the communications and the flight navigation computer and the ACARS transponder. The Pilot remaining in the cockpit has to manually take control of the aeroplane and is pulling the flight controls with both hands, with all his strength, back towards his lap, in an attempt to pull the nose of the aeroplane back up, as he is aware that they are losing altitude at an alarming rate. The pilot in the toilet is in immediate mortal danger. There is no mask in the toilets and the decompression is so rapid he has no time to find a mask and falls unconscious within a very few seconds. The plastic passenger masks fall down in the passenger cabin within a second of the decompression event, and people would rush to put them on, anyone not wearing one has approximately thirteen seconds before they fall unconscious. The pilot wants to reach for his replacement oxygen masks but so sudden is the depressurisation event and so violently is the plane dropping from the sky that the pilot has to use all his strength immediately to hold the plane from plummeting into the South China Sea below. In a very short space of time – a matter of fifteen to twenty seconds – the oxygen is literally sucked from the captains lungs and he to falls unconscious. Some of the passengers and some of the cabin crew will have been quick enough in donning their masks and will, however, have survived the initial emergency. The flight attendants would attempt to establish contact with the flight deck to no avail.

There is however a more serious problem. The pilot has passed out at the controls and may even now be dead. The copilot has suffered the same fate. The stewards would now quickly realise that they would have to gain access to the cockpit immediately. Nearly all Chief Stewards know of a way to circumvent the Security door on a Boeing 777; the door locking mechanisms on the security doors on passenger airliners were revised and then changed after a Silk Air pilot may have locked the other pilot out of the cockpit whilst on the approach to Singapore Airport and then allegedly purposefully put the plane into a vertical dive and intentionally crashed it into a swamp in a suicide/murder. The ensuing investigation stating that it was too simple for one pilot to commandeer the cockpit with the cable locking system they were using at that time and that a different method of locking the doors should be found that would allow the doors to be bypassed if one flight crew member found himself locked out by the other.

This is an alarmingly simple procedure that takes about thirty seconds if you know what you are doing. I will deal at length with the technical details of how this is done later in this book, but I feel sure you will be amazed when you read how simple a procedure it is. Once the security door has been opened two people would need to climb into the pilot and copilots' seats and attempt to fly the aeroplane. Remember they would still be wearing their replacement air masks with pressurised air canisters attached to the front. These have a tendency to fog up as we have said before. The cabin stewards now flying the plane would know they were too low and would undoubtedly pull up on the flight controls. I think anyone would know to do this and it would be almost instinctive. The damage to the rear roof of the aeroplane is an uneven tear and is lying backward to the left or port side of the aeroplane, which is causing the aeroplane to fly to the left as if the rudder had been turned. This has gone un-noticed by the completely novice replacement pilots who are severely panicking. The plane stop descending and levels out and then begins to climb; it had dropped almost fifteen thousand feet in the initial emergency.

Climbing now though was every bit as serious as the first emergency. The passenger emergency, replacement air generator was just about depleted, as it can only generate air for ten minutes and then runs out, and the high altitude would be deadly for anyone not wearing an air masks with pressurised air cylinder attached. The flight had dropped a few thousand feet after the initial emergency as the hole in the fuselage had altered the aeroplanes flight characteristic and the increased drag had slowed the planes air speed. The efforts the dying pilot had made had saved the aeroplane from plummeting into the sea below, and the aeroplane had been levelled out by the cabin crew and was now climbing higher than it should. It may be that the new pilots did not know the correct height, it may be that they could not see properly out of their masks or were simply too stressed to notice amidst all the noise of alarms in the cockpit, but whatever reason they climbed and climbed up to 45,000 feet. Sadly the passengers' lives were lost because of this and the remainder of the cabin crew would perish soon after, the two new pilots utilising the pilot and copilots replacement air masks as they were not steamed up were oblivious to the death of everyone behind them, all strapped into their seats and wearing masks that offered no air.

It was only as they realised their own air would run out soon by the gauge on the tank beside them, that they worked out they would need to descend to find breathable air. Most qualified cabin crew know that the air pressure is sufficient to breath at 12,000 feet and would probably be able read an altimeter to find their way down there. By now though, they were hopelessly lost. The flight direction and altitudes confirmed to us by Malaysian and Thai radar would be followed, in this case by a hopelessly inexperienced pair of people, desperately trying to save their lives. They would descend down low to try and visually recognise a familiar landscape or any geological structure to help them identify their position and to try and help their plight; this would sadly be misconstrued as a more sinister act of trying to avoid radar, as opposed to a desperate attempt to find salvation. As in the previous scenario the cabin crew attempting to fly the plane without any kind of guidance equipment or radio communications to help them, and flying at night would be difficult a task for them to overcome, and I fear as in the case before they would have perished in the plane also. Having to fly at night with no navigation computer, no flight experience, no communication and the on board radar also smashed by the initial tear in the fuselage, thus leaving them with no accurate way of determining where they are. The only instruments they could use for navigation would be the compass and altimeter. The first thing they would notice is that they were flying due west and not north as they thought they should be. More disorientation. Then they would be faced with a dilemma. They don't know where they are, what is in front of them or below them. Remember at this point they are flying at 12,000 feet, and visibility is poor due to low cloud. They cannot climb higher to stop themselves from flying into mountains, as this may cause them to asphyxiate or at least turn hypoxic, as they are now completely out of emergency air rations, and they can't really descend to see what they can actually see with the naked eye below the cloud level as this would increase the chances of flying into mountains. However with no reference point to give them any kind of idea where they were, they would have to descend, and this is what the plane did. The radar data showed the flight dropped down to 5,000 feet. It may be that the flight had passed over the Malaysian mainland and was now over the

Andaman Sea, and the survivor piloting the plane may have thought they were still over the South China Sea, and then with a sense of relief decided to turn north, sure they would soon fly over either Vietnamese or Cambodian coastline, and from there they would follow the coast and probably hope to find their way to Ho Chi Minh City Airport.

Sadly the plane was in the Andaman Sea and north would take them away from land, and they may have flown up the centre of the Malacca Straits, which is a body of water wide enough that an aeroplane could fly up the centre of it at 5,000 feet without seeing land on either side. They may have relaxed slightly, as they felt confident that the coastline would appear if they continued on this flight path. After a half hour or so of northwards flying the person flying the aeroplane, by now completely confused and disoriented, would become hugely afraid, as they would realise they were hopelessly lost. This has killed many, many experienced pilots over the years and in a famous case, a squadron of American fighters flying from Florida became disoriented in exactly this way and they all ended up ditching in the sea somewhere near the point where the Gulf of Mexico meets the Atlantic Ocean, with all hands lost and no trace of the missing squadron ever found to this day.

Once the surviving cabin crew member realises this they decide to change direction, perhaps even beginning to question the accuracy of the compass and other equipment. They would turn west, away from the Andaman Sea and out over the Indian Ocean, although I feel sure they did not know this, I think they probably still thought they were in The South China Sea. Hopelessly disoriented and confused. Finally they would turn again, this time south, and I think this is significant. If the survivor felt they were in the South China Sea and wanted to find land they would turn west ... that is what most pilots would do and then they would hug the coast till they came across a landmark they recognised and then navigate from there.

However the survivor flying the plane tried this, and now would be desperate. The south turn is perfectly understandable, it may show desperation, and it may show the person flying the plane was helplessly lost, west then north then west then south ... at low level ... under cloud cover ... it does have the look of someone searching and this may have been the case. The survivor continued south, possibly now with a renewed determination that they must run across land at some time. Sadly they were wrong. This was their terribly unfortunate fate, and as the plane flew south over the Indian Ocean at 5,000 feet they scoured the sea below for signs of life and land, their efforts only succeeding in lengthening their suffering. Finally the aeroplanes fuel supply was exhausted and the engines cut out; one side first, and then, rolling towards that side as the lop sided power delivery was not compensated for, the plane flipped over and went into a steep descent, slowly at first, and then with gathering momentum and downward pitch. The final alarms now sounded for over-speed and terrain, and the plane plunged into the Indian Ocean. The remaining members of the crew had prolonged their lives by a few short, stressful hours, until the almost impossible position they had found themselves in caught up with them, and they shared the fate of their work colleagues and passengers.

Once again I feel this is a possibility. It covers every eventuality that we know as fact. The aeroplane does have a fault that could cause this, however, it was inspected only two weeks before and one would expect that flaw to have shown up then. The fact that it is a known fault would ensure it was closely looked at. Furthermore the timing of the ACARS being switched off is perhaps wrong, but it should be noted that the ACARS transponder only answers to a signal sent to it by radar stations, and it had answered the previous signal, it was out of radar range at that point the incident happened that caused it to turn, so it is perhaps a little early for anyone to state as fact that it was in fact switched off before the incident took place, it may well have been switched on still, but without a signal from a radar tower to answer to, as it was out of range of radar, then it would seem to be switched off, but in fact, was just waiting for a signal. It should be noted that if some time in the future this is shown to have been the case then I hope the pilots and crew receive as much praise then as criticism now.

There has been at least one instance where the flight crew perished due to decompression and at least one member of the cabin crew survived, and then died because he could not get into the cockpit and the plane was left pilotless. It is important for everyone to realise that these sudden decompression events are not like anything a normal person has ever experienced. The time a person has before he loses consciousness at high altitudes may be ten to twenty seconds – that is ten to twenty seconds from death in reality, as if you are unconscious you cannot put your mask on and no one else would really be in a position to help you. The cabin crew would not be able to lift a fully-grown man, and I am not being sexist, but the majority of them are women and men are very heavy.

In any event, they would have a very short space of time to get someone lifted up and a mask on him, before he was severely brain injured anyway, experts say this might be as short as sixty seconds. The reason it is so dangerous is that the breath is forcibly sucked from your lungs, not like fully exhaling, its more severe than that. So if you imagine exhaling all the air from your lungs and then attaching a vacuum cleaner to a mask covering your nose and throat, then you can imagine how desperately short of time you would be in order to get your emergency mask on. It would be incredibly difficult to try and hold your breath, and fly an aeroplane, and deal with the master alarms whilst finding your emergency air mask, many of which need the valve manually opened as well, and you might come somewhere close to understanding the kind of event that some pilots have had to deal with.

In the instance I have mentioned above the Federal Aviation Administration conducted its usual thorough investigation. These investigations are known around the world to be amongst the most difficult undertaken by any investigative body, due to the often harrowing initial scene of human destruction at the crash site and then on to the investigation which in many cases has little more than crumpled metal to go on.

Cockpit recorders and data recorders have no doubt helped these investigations, and in turn made flying safer as a consequence, but it was once described as the broken needle hunt in the crumpled haystack on the side of a mountain by the people working these cases.

The investigation into this crash showed odd marks on the cockpit safety door, specifically moon shaped indentations. The investigators did not feel that these were crash related marks and felt they had been done by someone on board after take-off and before the crash. So it transpired; the marks were from a fire extinguisher bottom that a survivor had used as a form of battering ram to try to break through the cockpit security door. A member of the cabin crew had been able to put on his compressed air cylinder mask in time, and had survived everyone else on the flight only to be locked out of the cockpit by the cockpit safety door. The poor man tried in vain, whilst he had oxygen to breath from the pressurised cylinder fed mask he had, and had scavenged from around the passenger cabin, to force his way into the cockpit so he could attempt to save himself. All his efforts were sadly not enough and he also died of asphyxiation, surrounded by the bodies of the others on the flight. This and the case I mentioned earlier led to a new system being advised, whereby crewmembers can in fact in, extreme emergencies, if they find themselves locked out of the cockpit, circumvent the safety door and gain access to the flight deck. There is in fact more than one way this can be achieved.

So it is possible that both of the pilots perished in this way, and it is possible a member of the flight crew survived. It is also probable that they would know how to circumvent the safety door. They would also know that they could not breathe at this altitude and would need to descend immediately, that the plane also did, and the fact that it descended to 12,000 feet is actually very compelling as that is the height that pilots are told to descend to in these decompression emergency situations, and any trained cabin crew member would know that number, they would know 12,000 feet for sure. So for me that is a fair indicator that,

A. there was a decompression event and,
B. whoever was flying knew that at twelve thousand feet they would be safe from that.

When you add both of those factors together and add that your average layman would not know to descend to 12,000 feet, but someone in the flight crew or cabin staff probably would, you get the feeling that there may have been someone from the crew flying when the plane descended.

Some might say it would take the perfect storm of bad luck for the structural fault to overload the electrical systems on the aeroplane and switch off the ACARS and the communications but I'm also saying it is not impossible. Improbable perhaps, but let us not forget we are involved in an air crash incident where a plane full of people has vanished completely without trace, for no apparent reason; and that is about as improbable as it comes, so I am going to say that something highly unlikely must have happened somewhere along the line. If I had asked anyone reading this, prior to the disappearance of Flight MH 370, if there was any chance an aeroplane full of people, and one of the most reliable and safe models of aeroplane that had ever been built, at that, under the control of a highly respected and experienced Captain and able and popular copilot, could vanish as this one has done, I would have been laughed at.

So let us not talk about improbabilities. It WAS possible, and if MH 370 went missing in the way this scenario says and left an untrained cabin crew member flying the aeroplane, then the cabin crew member that tried to fly the aeroplane was a human being, and history has shown, that under these extremes of stress and fear, humans never perform well, regardless of how well they are trained. Yes training helps, and can prepare the mind and body for dealing with emergencies, but the person left flying had not been trained for this scenario.

All of the movements that the aeroplane made could tie in with the radar information that we have been given. The survivor at the controls would be incredibly stressed, and undoubtedly disoriented. Cabin crews, by and large, only have a slight idea of where they are during a flight, in relation to cities and mountains and seas and oceans and of course this knowledge will vary from person to person. With the navigation computer off and the communications also not functioning they would have found themselves in a very confusing situation.

There would have to have been an incredible amount of bad luck for this to have happened as suggested but I will leave that decision up to you.

Now there is another scenario – it is possible that either the pilot of the aeroplane that night Captain Shah, or the copilot, Fariq Hamid, whilst acting either individually, or together, or with others on board whose identities are as yet unknown, hijacked the aeroplane and flew it on a route they had designed with very careful timing, with the specific intention of avoiding commercial radar. The hijackers needed to avoid radar detection from the moment of hijack, in order to hide the aeroplane, in the hope of not having the hijack discovered so they could use the aeroplane as a human guided missile, just as the terrorists had done in New York, and crash the plane into the British overseas territory island called Diego Garcia.

The Island of Diego Garcia is leased to the United States Military and is in constant use. In fact it is amongst the busiest air bases the U.S. Military operate. The Island possesses a very long runway, capable of handling the huge B52 bombers, and the U.S. military uses it to fly bombing missions, resupply missions, and covert operations to Afghanistan, The Yemen, Somalia, North Pakistan and previously also in Iraq. The island is also home to a large deployment of CIA personnel, and when the U.S. were allegedly indulging in state sanctioned torture of suspected Jihadist terrorists and individuals captured in battle – extraordinary rendition as it was called then – much of it was believed to have been done by CIA operatives hidden away on this remote Island. The Island is a vital piece of the U.S. Military's global reach capability. The Middle East countries are within five hours flying time and the Islands' remoteness offers a great natural defence from enemy attack. It is one of the most densely populated places on Planet Earth per square foot, with a complement of at least three thousand personnel. These range from cooks to airforce aeroplane service personnel, drone engineers, CIA people, Military Pilots, basically a full cross section of the military personnel required to man an active airbase. The island is totally developed and there are buildings over a large part of its entire footprint, with the exception of the runway. Undoubtedly this would be a major prize for any Jihadist that had the ability to take a flight and reach there, as so long as the plane was crashed into any building and not the runway the loss of American life would be significant. The added value of destroying some of the USA's military capability would also be a plus.

I also believe that if this was the case, and Jihadists did in fact hijack the flight with the intention of attacking the base at Diego Garcia, they would never have been able to achieve the attack, as the American Military would have tracked Flight MH 370 from the moment its transponder was switched off. I will later in this book show how they tracked this aeroplane. This would have led to an extremely delicate and fraught few hours for the President of the United States, Barrack Obama, as the flight path that MH 370 was taking, would very early on betray the intentions and the intended target of the Jihadists on board, as Diego Garcia stands alone in that body of water hundreds of miles from any other Island.

The terrorists may have wrongly believed that the U.S. Military did not have the capabilities to track a passenger aeroplane that was flying low, below the height that it would be visible to radar, and that had its transponder turned off. If Jihadists had hijacked MH 370 it would have been shot down by the Americans before it reached Diego Garcia. I believe the plane may have been shot down within the territorial waters of the islands by the U.S. Military so they would have total control of the crash site, without the risk of any foreign ships or aeroplanes finding the debris as would happen in the open ocean.

I will later show that there is absolutely no way this plane could have disappeared, and that I believe the Americans knew on the 8 March – the same day the plane had taken off – exactly where it had gone into the water. I also believe that the Americans told the Malaysian Prime Minister almost immediately what had happened, and that he also confirmed to him that sadly everyone on board was killed that night.

The aeroplane may have been shot down within the territorial waters of the islands, which is an enormous area of deep water, which would extend under normal circumstances twelve nautical miles from the shore line of the Island, but as this is a military base the Americans have extended this maritime exclusion zone significantly further into the Indian Ocean, and in fact hold command of the sea an area almost 200 nautical miles from the islands edges.

Flight MH 370 like every other passenger aeroplane on planet earth, would have been tracked by an international Internet company from the moment it took off from Kuala Lumpur, throughout every part of its flight, right up until the point the ACARS transponder was switched off. FlightRadar 24.com is a Swedish Internet Company that administers a site that tracks, in real-time, civilian aeroplane as they fly around the globe. Flightaware.co.uk is another such site that does the same and regularly tracks 4,000 or more aeroplanes that are airborne at the same time and have an enormous database of historic flights with more than three hundred and sixty-six million recorded flights. These sites use the data the ACARS transponder on an aeroplane sends to radar stations to keep an accurate record of all flight positions throughout their journey. Flight MH 370 was tracked by these sites that night until the transponder stopped working, or as I believe was switched off.

The U.S. Military monitor these sites and the moment and aeroplane misses an ACARS transponder message it is immediately red flagged, and the U.S. Military would use its covert satellite based tracking system to positively track the aeroplane from that moment on. The aeroplane may have been intentionally shot down as it approached the hijackers target of Diego Garcia, whereby it fell into the Indian Ocean into the area of water which is heavily protected by the US Military, and not in International waters, which are heavily fished by large fishing vessels from many international countries, so that no fishing trawlers would stumble upon the debris from the downed flight, and no other shipping or aeroplanes could approach the crash site.

I also believe, that everyone else on board, other than whoever was piloting the aeroplane, and perhaps one other, would have, sadly already been dead prior to the plane being shot down, and that they had been intentionally murdered by the Jihadist or Jihadists that had hijacked the aeroplane, by first switching the cabin pressurisation switch from auto to manual, and thus depressurising the entire aeroplane and secondly, flying the aeroplane up to its ceiling height of 45,000 feet and waiting there for more than twenty minutes, until all the emergency replacement oxygen, both in the passengers' drop down masks and the cabin crews pressurised cylinder masks was exhausted. These in fact would have been completely exhausted after only ten minutes but the hijackers may have chosen to remain so high for another ten minutes or so to ensure everyone was dead even if they had managed to find themselves another cylinder mask.

MH370 – FOLLOW THE LIES TO GET TO THE TRUTH

The utter callousness and disregard for human life in this mission almost beggars belief.

Undoubtedly any decision to shoot an unarmed civilian passenger airliner out the sky would be a decision that could only be made at the highest level, so President Obama would have to have made it, if this scenario is correct. If this is indeed what happened then I firmly believe that the President had no choice to make in the matter, the aeroplane would have to be shot down, and no blame should be apportioned to him because of this decision.

If this is in fact what happened to the aeroplane, then The U.S. Military, President Obama and the Malaysian Government have concealed this from the world at large. I will discuss possible motivations for this later. The Malaysian Prime Minister has I believe lied and deceived from the start to manipulate this situation for political gain. I believe I can show this.

The mortal remains of the murdered passengers and crew from Flight MH 370, and as much debris as was humanly possible to find and recover, would have to have been collected from the waters by the CIA. It could be there is an ongoing operation by the CIA to move the human remains and the collected aeroplane debris to another location. It may be that they never intend to allow them to be found. The object of either of these most macabre operations would be to deceive the world, and to give the American Military and the American President the ability to firstly deny, and then secondly prove, they never shot Flight MH 370 down.

There would be a very good reason for the Americans wanting to deny they shot the aeroplane down, apart from the obvious one that is of course, that they shot down an aeroplane full of innocent civilians, who may have still been alive in the aeroplane at that time. The reason would be that they have done exactly the same before, that is, shoot a passenger jet full of people out of the sky, and the retribution brought against innocent Americans as a direct result of that mistake then, was quite horrendous, and they did not want another such attack on their civilians as a result of this disaster.

The US Military and President Obama may have in fact concealed the shooting down of this aeroplane for more than one reason. We can explore the other reasons later in this book, but they might be considered by some, to be even more compelling.

Disinformation from a number of collaborating sources has delayed the proper search, by using a series of red herrings. There was satellite images showing debris in many different parts of the Southern Ocean, and to this day, not one piece has been recovered. The search was moved around the Southern Ocean by these images, five hundred miles further north, then a thousand miles south, then back north, with the position being constantly changed. Many times the searchers were sent these huge distances in boats and did no searching at all as they spent their whole time repositioning from one search sector to another. In fact as the search progressed in the Southern Ocean the Chinese became so disillusioned with the search organisation they broke away from the Australian organised search and began to look much further north. This constant repositioning was done to give the impression of a frantic search, but I believe it was in fact a stalling tactic and done to buy time.

Of all the red herrings the searchers were being given though, the biggest and most cynical piece of deception was in my opinion given was by the Malaysian transport Minister Hishammuddin Hussein. You see Minister Hussein is in fact the Minister of Defence and has been for some time; in fact he only took on the job as Transportation Minister a few days before this unfortunate incident took place, as the previous Minister had resigned his post at short notice. Minister Hussein then, was in the perfect position to be able to access BOTH civilian and military radar that night. We have been told that it was almost an hour after the final communication from the flight that the Vietnamese Air Traffic Control realised that Flight MH 370 had not contacted them as it entered their jurisdiction, and that it had in fact disappeared from radar as well, and they raised the alarm by contacting Malaysian Air Traffic Control. We have also subsequently been told that Malaysian military radar tracked the flight from its final communication position at 01.19am, back across the Malaysian peninsula, close to the border with Thailand and out into the Malacca Sea – So why did the Malaysian Transport/Defence Minister Hussein send the search parties to the South China Sea first thing on the morning of 8 March? He would undoubtedly have been told by the Military radar he commands, that the flight went west out into the Malacca Straits. So why look in the South China Sea?

It was a full twenty-four hours later that they began to search in the Malacca Straits. Now I could understand if he sent search crews to both areas simultaneously, just in case there was some wrong information and he wanted to cover any eventuality, but he did not. Remember the searchers were meant to be looking for survivors according to Minister Hussein, and he simply did not send anyone to the point the aeroplane last appeared on his radar. There can be only one explanation in my opinion for his actions, he sent the search party to the South China Sea first, knowing that he would be sending them to the Malacca Straights the next day so he and his Government could buy time and they needed time to cover their tracks.

The fact that the Government in Malaysia may have chosen to follow America into this lie will no doubt sound almost unbelievable to some people, however, I think I can show a very compelling reason for this and, also expose them for one of the most politically cynical character assassinations I have ever witnessed, and they did it for political gain. Proof if ever needed that absolute power corrupts absolutely. The United States Government carries much strength financially and has also considerable political power around the world. They have shown in the past that they have the ability to corrupt most politicians and to influence foreign Governments, as America is the biggest Military, and biggest single market in the world. They can offer foreign Governments promises of support against other nations that they perhaps have disagreements with. They can offer military aid and support. They can offer enormous contracts that can help secure large numbers of jobs. In short, they have a very wide array of superb bargaining counters with which to coerce and convince foreign governments, and their officials, to do the bidding of the United States.

If this scenario is correct then I think the US President would have phoned the Malaysian Prime Minister Razak and explained to him what had just happened to Flight MH 370 and then they would have decided between them the best course of action from that point on. There can be no doubt that the Malaysians Government officials knew from the very first moment what had happened to the aeroplane that night, as they sent the search crews to the wrong search site in the South China Sea that very morning, and they never sent rescuers to the Malacca Straights. This can possibly be explained by the fact that they already knew the fate that had befallen MH 370, had they not know what had happened they would have sent rescuers to both areas to look for survivors , in my opinion.

The Government in Malaysia has been in power since 1963 and has been re-elected routinely ever since then. They have, until the last set of elections, never faced any creditable political opposition, however at the most recent election they were run very close by the opposition party, and were very nearly beaten. For this party to have lost would have been a disaster, as any politician will tell you, that the longer the people are in charge of a political situation the less respect they have for the rules. In short, if they had lost the election, there is a good chance the new Government might have uncovered a wide array of very serious offences and misappropriations. There is certain proof of this, because the ruling party, under the leadership of Prime Minister Razak have managed to manipulate the legal system sufficiently to have the opposition party leader jailed for five years on what is widely believed to be trumped up charges. The classic case of a dictator removing the opposition's voice, so his is the only one left that can be heard.

This flight was in fact being flown that night by Captain Shah, who by an amazing twist of fate is actually related to the Opposition Party leader, who had that very day been put in jail. Captain Shah was in fact a fervent political supporter of his relative and helped him in his political campaigning. The Malaysian Government, acting with the Americans, seized the opportunity to parcel this missing flight and the blame for its disappearance, on to the shoulders of Captain Shah, happy in the knowledge that they could then use him as a political pawn to help further discredit his relation, the Opposition Party leader. They have told us he was mentally disturbed, that he was recently separated from his wife and that he was probably suicidal. Even though his wife and sons fervently denied this was the case. In my opinion they have maligned his name without a shred of evidence.

We were constantly told that the flight had two black box recorders, specifically the cockpit voice recorder, and the flight data recorder. Some more modern aeroplanes have these two pieces of equipment combined, but on an aeroplane of this type they are separate. Each of these black boxes has a 'pinger' noise generator on them that are battery operated and built to survive the impact of an aeroplane crash. The 'pings' it sends out are to help searchers pinpoint the position of the black boxes in the event of a crash. The batteries are kept charged by the aeroplane whilst in normal use, and the batteries had a lifespan, once switched on, of approximately four weeks. The 'black boxes' were automatically switched on once they were submerged in water. This then set the time scale for the search for the black boxes of flight MH 370. The constant moving of the search locations by the Malaysians was done I believe to buy time, perhaps so the crash debris of the shot down aeroplane could be gathered, and also horrifically, to recover the corpses of the murdered passengers. They would also need to find the black boxes of Flight MH 370, and this would have given them a serious problem that they needed time for; time that they would need to generate by misleading the actual search.

This would be a relatively straight forward task as the Malaysians would have been happy to follow the Americans' lead in this matter and all information being made public regarding MH 370 was being done by the Malaysians. If this scenario is correct then the aeroplane had in fact crashed into deep water, and the only piece of equipment that could find the black boxes in this difficult environment by locating their positions from the 'pings' they gave off, was the deep water 'pinger' locator, of which only one exists in the world.

This is a state of the art piece of equipment is towed behind a ship by a very long steel cable, allowing it to get down to a depth from which it can detect the 'pings' on its sensitive acoustic array. This would be a slight problem for the CIA as they put in place information, that once found, would point the searchers to a very inhospitable part of the world where the water was very, very deep, and once the search crews got there they would be sure to ask the US Government for the very 'pinger' locator the CIA would need themselves at the actual crash site to find the same black boxes. It may be the case that the Americans then intended to drop the black boxes into the depth of the location southwest of Australia to help convince the world beyond any reasonable doubt that that was in fact where the plane had come down. It is one theory that the black boxes, may have in fact, been recovered by the CIA at the Diago

Garcia crash site, and virtually the whole time the search was going on in the southern ocean, were in their possession. These would then be used to confirm to the world that the flight went down in the Southern Ocean once it had run out of fuel after a deranged member of the flight crew hijacked it for his own personal reasons. This would be done primarily to exonerate the United States and its President from the killing of an aeroplane full of innocent people. There were other reasons why they chose to hide this from the world, and I will deal with them in depth later.

This may sound an almost incredible scenario, and at the outset I felt it unlikely myself, but once you try to apportion behaviour, and understand why lies were told, it becomes more and more acceptable. One event is very compelling in my mind, and I think you may find it likewise. Either way the facts may show they were at least feasible. The fact that at the most important stage of the search for the black boxes in deep water southwest of Australia, when the most critically important piece of equipment was the towed array pinger locator, when time was of the utmost importance to locate the black boxes before the batteries ran out, the Americans put the towed array locator on a ship to transport it to Perth Australia. It is the size of a dining room table and not heavy. It seems more logical to have put this on an aeroplane to get it on site as quickly as possible to maximise the chances of finding the missing aeroplane. Yet they put it on the slowest possible means of transport they could. It could be construed that there was a concerted effort to delay the search by this action. This may just be another hypothetical scenario that successfully deals with all the factual information we have been given to date, but also, more importantly, deals with all the lies we have been told. I feel it exposes the truths these lies tell, and explains the real reason we were told them in the first place.

From day one in the case of Malaysian flight MH 370, I, like many other people felt that it was an impossibility for a jet liner full of people to vanish anywhere on this planet without some form of radar or satellite tracking or GPS indication as to its whereabouts ... I contend that I, and everyone else who felt the same, was correct. I believe it is impossible for an aeroplane full of people to disappear. The plane was tracked from very early on until it crashed and here is the proof.

The cold war gave the world many things ... too many nuclear warheads being one, and intercontinental ballistic missiles that carried them being another. For reasons of self-preservation the United States Government – correctly in my opinion – decided they needed an early warning system to give themselves enough time to react to a pre-emptive strike from the Russians with their Inter Continental Ballistic Missiles or ICBMs. This was a superb deterrent to anyone foolhardy enough to launch an attack on the US mainland or its Allies. The thinking being that once the Inter Continental Missile, or ICBM, attack had been launched the early warning system would detect it and then before the Russian missiles had arrived on to American soil, the US and its NATO Treaty allies would respond with their own ICBM missiles, both sets of missiles passing each other flying in opposite directions, leaving both countries destroyed and the planet more or less uninhabitable. It basically made the possibility of winning a war with nuclear weapons impossible and thus made the weapons unusable.

The early warning system itself required that the scientists working for the US military design a system capable of detecting the heat signature given off by the Russian ICBM rocket motors at the moment of launch, and then the ability to track these missiles through their flight path, which is actually in sub-orbital space, through their re-entry into earths' atmosphere and onto their eventual detonation target. The system was designed and built and deployed. A large number of detection and tracking satellites were sent into orbit covering every inch of the planet, including both Poles. The headquarters and command centre of this system would need to be in a tremendously hardened safe structure, and so the US Military built the incredible Cheyenne Mountain Complex at El Paso County in Colorado – an iconic structure, and testimony to how serious the threat of nuclear war was back then. It is basically a hollowed out granite mountain. It is quite breathtakingly enormous inside, complete with blast doors and it even has a fully functioning hospital. This is where the U.S. Military based NORAD, America's strategic nuclear missile defence.

From this complex the early warnings would be received and word would immediately be passed to the President who would then issue the order to retaliate. The Presidents orders to launch would have been directed from Cheyenne Mountain to all the different arms of the US Military nuclear defence. The early warning system has amazing capabilities, and is able to detect a ballistic missile launch anywhere in the world, as I said before, including both poles and it can detect these missiles almost immediately the rocket motors are ignited, virtually as they are leaving their launch silos, or from the backs of the mobile launchers. Americas strategic nuclear defence also relied on submarine launched ICBMs, which used stealth as its primary defence, and the Strategic airborne deterrent. The airborne deterrent being significant in the case of the missing Malaysian flight and this is why.

The American Strategic Air Deterrent was B52 bombers, armed with nuclear bombs. These are very high speed and reliable aircraft that are capable of carrying large payloads of up to thirty-two tonnes. Latterly they carried nuclear-armed cruise missiles, although before this technology existed they in fact carried 'dumb' nuclear bombs that were delivered onto target by pilot skill and gravity alone. Numbers vary but generally there were eighty-five of these planes under the control of the Strategic Air Command, or SAC, as it was known.

The deterrent required that fully loaded and armed with nuclear weapons, these bombers would take off and fly up over the Arctic Circle. Once there they would circle for endless hours and wait for the order to attack. The B52s were refuelled in air and would hold their station there for hours on end until they were relieved by the replacement B52s. The SAC kept aeroplanes aloft, circling, waiting for the call to attack, twenty-four hours a day every day of the year, without exception, for years on end. The Russians did the same, and these Russian aeroplanes were tracked by the satellite early warning system at Cheyenne Mountain. This system has been improved over the years and was adapted after the September the eleventh attacks so that it could accurately track any aeroplane anywhere around the globe that the US felt was a threat, either military or civilian, in order to give early warning, especially in the case of a hijack. This system would have tracked Flight MH 370 from the moment it switched its transponder off. In recent years the tracking capability and warning station has been moved a short distance from Cheyenne Mountain to underground bunkers at Paterson Air Force Base.

If further proof this system actually does exist is needed it, then this is easily verified. If this system did not exist and the Russians or Chinese wanted to attack America then they would not need ICBMs or submarine borne nuclear missiles, they would simply covertly load a nuclear warhead into the hold of a number of passenger, or commercial aeroplanes that were heading to America, and there are hundreds each day, and once the aeroplane had entered the US airspace the pilots, on a suicide mission very similar to that of the B52 Bomber pilots, would simply switch off the aeroplanes transponders and fly low to pre-designated targets throughout the US to deliver their nuclear payload, and the US Military would have been impotent to protect themselves from this. In my opinion they already have the technology in space anyway.

Subsequent to the cold war being brought to an end and the threat of nuclear Armageddon more or less being shelved, the capabilities were expanded to help in the search for earth crossing meteors, space rocks, and comets, and it can detect very small space rocks indeed – it is now also responsible for the tracking and mapping of all space objects orbiting around our planet. These include items as small as a spanner dropped by an astronaut on an early space walk. There are more than six million pieces of man-made material orbiting our planet, ranging from full satellites which are generally about the size of a family car, to the international space station which is the size of a small football pitch, to tiny pieces of destroyed satellites the size of a fist, and the Cheyenne complex knows the position of every one. This is necessary as, it was responsible for directing the space shuttle launch into an area of space that doesn't contain anything it could crash into, as this debris and usable stuff is moving very, very, fast – at speeds of twenty thousand miles an hour or more. The space shuttle had regularly been instructed to reposition once in orbit by the Cheyenne Mountain Complex in order to avoid collision with other space items, this is a fairly common occurrence, so as you can imagine; it is a pretty sensitive array. This system has been improved upon over the years and was adapted once again after the September the eleventh attacks to passively track every aeroplane flying around the globe in order to give accurate early warning in case of hijack. This system would have tracked Flight MH 370 from the moment the aeroplane transponder was switched off. To suggest that an aeroplane would go untracked by Cheyenne Mountain is utter nonsense.

I can further prove this. If I take you back to that horrendous day on September the eleventh, the day that terrorists hijacked a series of aeroplanes and used them as human guided missiles to attack strategic targets around America. On that day the terrorists all switched off the aeroplane transponders and then flew low in a ground hugging fashion to avoid radar. Do you remember Cheyenne Mountain speaking directly to air traffic control about the position of the aeroplanes that had been hijacked? The system operator clearly asking if this was 'a simulation or real world' the conversations that day are in fact a matter of public record and were highlighted by the 9/11 Commission into the attacks and the report suggested a system be implemented to track aircraft in American airspace.

The early warning tracking system was adapted to do this and as it had global reach was deemed, by the American NSA, as sensible to keep an eye out on all aeroplanes worldwide, Military and commercial. Any plane flying around the world that switched off its ACARS Transponder would immediately be identified by the tracking system computers as being potentially hijacked. The 9/11 attackers did just that and if you believe the American Military and Government would leave this obvious hole in their defences open for a second time, you are crazy. The terrorists on that day in fact turned passenger aeroplanes into human guided stealth missiles. The irony of this is that on that day they may well have done the United States of America one of its biggest favours ever.

Let me explain; you see the attacks on that day highlighted and exploited a huge gap in Americas defences, namely that whilst a hostile enemy military aeroplane or missile could not go undetected in an attack on the USA, a passenger jet, either commercial, private or chartered, could in fact very easily hide in plain sight, if you pardon the pun. Imagine if a foreign country had wanted to attack America with nuclear weapons hidden in some of the thousands of commercial jets that fly into America every day. They could have behaved exactly as the jihadists did on that day but instead detonated nuclear warheads above strategic targets instead of crashing the aeroplanes. In fact using the aeroplanes as a human guided nuclear missile; again hidden in plain sight. In fact as we now know these aeroplanes can be pre-programmed to fly these routes without human help … they would not even necessarily require a pilot. It is the perfect 'fire and forget' weapons system, and there are thousands flying in and out of American airspace every day. This could have decapitated Americas nuclear deterrent and leadership and rendered them defenceless and defeated without firing a shot – leaving them open to any and all attack.

So the irony is absolute, the jihadists in their hate filled attack may well have highlighted the one way America could have been defeated militarily, they may well have saved America from an enormous attack by executing their own small minded attack. Make no mistake the Americans have firmly shut this gateway as a means of attack, and the worldwide tracking of all large jet airliners is the only way they could achieve this.

Further to the point of transponders. All military aircraft have transponders on them as well. This is so they can be tracked during peacetime. These transponders are switched off when the aircraft are taking off on a military operation, otherwise enemy transponder detectors would be able to pin-point the aircrafts exact position and intercept them. Theses transponders however are switched back on by the pilots once the aeroplane has left enemy territory, this is to identify themselves to friendly radar so it does not engage them as potential enemy aeroplanes and shoot them down. This weapon system can identify and track aeroplanes that have their transponders switched off, it was specifically designed to do this. A tragic case at the outset of the second Gulf War where an American fighter/bomber was engaged by the US Military missile defence battery that was stationed at the Iraqi border with Kuwait, it was thought to be Iraqi as the Pilot had failed to switch on his transponder which would have identified the aircraft to the missile's computer as friendly. Sadly on this occasion the pilot paid the ultimate price for his mistake.

The fact the U.S. Government has never released the whereabouts of the missing aeroplane is significant. They have routinely denied they have the capability to track aeroplanes such as this worldwide and in fact they denied they had the capability regarding this specific flight, MH 370. The Americans could not give the correct location of the aeroplane if it was at Diego Garcia as it would be too apparent that this was the intended target, and they could not give an accurate position of a false site as the searchers would go there and find no wreckage. I believe the truth is it is not that the Americans cannot give the position of the missing aeroplane; it is that they will not. They would not say where the aeroplane was, because they needed time to organise their subterfuge. So they were left with the only option, which was to stay silent and deny that they had the ability to track an aeroplane with its transponder switched off.

Make no mistake, the Flight Tracker civilian company tracked Flight MH 370 passively that night, just as the computer system is designed to do with every aeroplane, but the moment that plane left Malaysian air space and the ACARS transponder was switched off and then failed to contact Vietnamese Air Traffic Control a red flag would have gone up. Then the plane would be actively watched by the Paterson bunker complex operator. The people working there have a very high security clearance and are used to being tight lipped about anything they see or hear. I believe that the systems in the Paterson bunker complex could very easily pinpoint to within a couple of metres exactly where the plane went down, and they haven't said a word ... because they've been told not to, in order to cover up what really happened. Everyone that works there has very high security clearance as I say, and would never discuss anything they see there, as the jail sentences in America are huge for anyone breaching Government or Military security.

All the Oceans around the planet are full of man-made debris. Both the Atlantic and Pacific Oceans have an enormous amount, in particular with an estimated half billion tonnes of man-made debris floating around in them, ranging from plastic bags to shipping containers, with some of the rubbish forming such large areas of gunk that shipping is instructed to sail around them, and the Indian Ocean and Southern oceans are no different, and yet we are expected to believe that no less than five Governments to date have re-tasked their spy satellites, an enormously difficult and time consuming task, to look for debris in the Southern Ocean – you don't need a satellite for that – you actually can't miss it, and the oceans are so vast and the resolution necessary to pinpoint something worthwhile so tight it would take years and years for human eyeballs to go over the data the military spy satellites produced ... and that just seems like a way of getting everyone to waste their time and efforts to me.

Speaking of wasting time let us look at the black boxes, or cockpit data recorder and cockpit voice recorder devices, which we have been told repeatedly have an active battery powered acoustic 'pinger' which is activated on contact with water and lasts for four weeks. The US Military has taken the decision to permanently station nuclear attack submarines in the Indian Ocean. It has done this for a number of reasons; as a defensive deterrent for both Diego Garcia and to protect the northeastern seaboard of Australia from potential attack from Indonesians, as for many years they have threatened an invasion, and as a reserve for the fifth Fleet which operates in the Arabian Gulf waters just off the Iranian coast. The acoustic capabilities of these submarines in water is really staggering, they can hear other submarines from many hundreds and sometimes thousands of miles away, and enemy submarines don't exactly advertise their presence. They are designed and built almost exclusively with silent operating in mind and are thus very quiet, so the listening capabilities of these submarines has to be very acute by consequence, and it is reasonable to assume that if a black box recorder was pinging away in the Indian Ocean or the Southern Ocean then for sure the attack sub would hear it, in fact I do not think they could miss it, and again the U.S. Military have not said a word.

Also a fairly surprising act by the US Navy caught my attention, the fact that they removed the one ship it had in the Southern Ocean that was helping with the sea search as early as 18 March after it had in fact only been on station for a few days. contend if the US Government were seriously looking for survivors in the water and let us not forget there were American citizens on board

MH 370, then there is no way that boat would have been ordered to withdraw. Imagine if survivors went into the water with one of them being an American and they had been abandoned by their own Navy and left to be rescued by a foreign countries ship, I think there would be an outcry in the US. They removed the Navy vessel they had there, as I think they knew it was a pointless search, as they obviously knew where the plane had been shot down. Look at the number of ships the Chinese have looking for the wreckage and potential survivors, dozens of them now, And America removed the one they had supposedly searching the crash site; I find that hard to swallow.

After the war on terror had begun in earnest and the US Military realised it could not keep track of so many potential enemy targets on the ground by using spy satellites alone, as these are very difficult to reposition and difficult to organise at short notice. Basically they needed an aviation platform that they could attach a very high resolution camera to, and preferably one that could stay in the air for long hours, in an area of conflict, without having to put a pilot in the constant way of harm. When unmanned drones were first used the Military were somewhat underwhelmed, they had no weapon capability and had limited range. As this technology has developed however, they have proven to be one of the most capable weapons platforms and useful stealthy information gatherers known to man. The modern drones can carry a relatively large weapons payload and can be controlled by pilots in real time, from an airbase in mainland USA by utilising a satellite uplink to send the control signals through. The cameras they have now are incredible and can read newspaper headlines from 50,000 feet up in altitude. They also have infrared cameras, and can stay aloft for many hours. They can be programmed to take off and fly to a target area, and then fly a grid pattern to search the whole area and then return to base and land itself. They really are an amazing piece of kit and if you were searching an enormous piece of ocean and looking for plane wreckage it would almost seem that these drones were designed for the job. They are the perfect searching tool for this job. These very advanced, pilotless aircraft are able to stay airborne for up to seven times the length of time as a conventional aircraft, and as they are unmanned no lives would be risked in a search using these, no small thing given the remoteness of the search area where an emergency on board any of the search aeroplanes might even spell death for the aeroplanes crew. They can even fly autonomously and would be able to fly many different grid patterns over a designated search area ... and guess what; The US Military have them stationed on Diego Garcia. Surely if the US Government was making a determined effort to search for the missing aircraft as you think they would be doing, then these would be deployed almost immediately ... the fact they haven't could perhaps suggest they are in fact not actually looking for it, but merely giving the impression that they are looking for it, and only one conclusion can be drawn from this. They are not actually looking for it because they already know where it is.

The fact that the search crews were pointed in the direction of the Southern Ocean is also an anomaly to me. I believe the satellite being used to verify the potential wreck sites of the aircraft was a communication satellite and not any part of any tracking array. As the satellites title suggests it was designed for communication and not tracking and the fact that an entirely unproven technology was used to attempt to pinpoint the missing plane's final destination, and that so much stock was put on the results of the unproven results, actually amazes me. It would seem an almost perfect way to trick people into searching in the wrong place. If Flight MH 370 is not found there is the perfect excuse already in place by saying it was an untried technology. This is also in fact the perfect place to 'lose' an aeroplane ... the deepest part of the ocean being considerably more than 8,000 metres deep, and with the vast majority of the seabed being more than four thousand five hundred metres deep, overall it is vastly deep body of water, with trenches and undersea mountainous areas.

Not to mention the fact that the prevailing wind, known as the 'roaring forties', which gets its name from its constant strength, and whips the sea in this area, almost constantly, into mountainous crests and troughs and is unmanageable for all but the largest ships. It is also one of the remotest spots on the planet with hardly even a small island in its midst. Anyone with an agenda that needed to make the job of searching for a missing plane so difficult for authorities, that they would waste enormous amounts of time doing the searching, would undoubtedly try and send them to that location to search ... this would be the spot I would pick ... coincidence? Almost incredibly the searches were halted in every other location on the strength of the word from the scientist working at Inmarsat, despite this being an untried technology and none of the scientists having been involved in forensic data analysis before.

There is a system now developed for tracking aeroplanes by satellites that has been developed as a commercial venture. It is called The Automatic Dependent Surveillance Broadcast, or ADS-B. It is a system that the US Aviation Board has refused to implement as they feel 'they don't need it'. I believe the reason they don't need it is because they already have it. This commercial system has been on the market for some time now.

Chapter 3

Hijack

Let us look at the possibilities of hijack. This is where no flight crew members were involved, and would be perpetrated by a passenger or passengers acting together to take control of the plane.

The first thing we should look at is the possible motivation for a hijack. There must obviously be a significant reason for such an extreme act and we shall look at these more closely here.

1. Mentally unstable person.

The kind of planning necessary to take this plane is pretty extensive; however we should not use this reason alone to discredit this hijack. The Columbine High School killers, who were two young men that shared a suicidal/murderous pact to attack their own school with the intention of killing as many fellow students as they could, were able to completely fool everyone in their lives that they were relatively normal kids and never once allowed their emotions to betray the horrendous act they were planning. They spent many months planning this mass murder, and in fact, it was planned almost like a military operation. This shows that people with the notion to perpetrate these horrendous acts can still operate amongst normally behaved people without raising suspicions and that they are capable of the kind of intricate planning necessary to carry out these deeds.

Firstly order of business for anyone attempting to hijack an passenger aeroplane is that they need to take control of the cockpit, and to achieve this they would need to defeat the security door which separates the passenger areas and the cockpit itself. This act alone would prove challenging if not impossible for a lone assailant, however, there is a possibility that this could be achieved, if say, one of the flight crew needed to access the passenger area in order to use the toilet. There is an accepted protocol in place now that is used by every commercial airline should the need arise for a member of the flight crew to leave the cockpit. This is in fact a fairly common occurrence.

The accepted protocol goes like this; a member of the cabin crew, having been called forward by either the pilot or copilot by using the two way phone that connects the forward galley with the cockpit, stands outside the door before it is opened from the inside. They are taught to survey the passengers in the immediate area near to the door, which can be the forward galley area, and the passenger area nearest to the cockpit, which is usually the first class area. Once they have signalled that they believe there is no perceived threat, either by the telephone that is immediately outside the cockpit door, or by signalling back to the camera that the pilots have pointed at this area, whoever is opening the door then checks in his camera monitor and once he concurs that there is no threat the door is released. The flight crew open the steel door from inside the cockpit by pressing a release button that is located between the two pilot's seats, it is an outward opening steel door with an electro-magnetic lock. The door itself is an immensely strong design and is tested rigorously to ensure it cannot be defeated even by very determined attackers that are armed with hand tools, and that have a considerable length of time to attack the door, the door shuts into a steel frame and it is said cannot be defeated even with an axe being wielded by a fit strong man. Once the person leaving the cockpit is outside the door it is then closed and locks itself automatically. The attending cabin crew waits at the door until the flight crew personnel returns, at which time they repeat the survey and once they have again established no threat use the telephone to ask for the door to be opened. Some flights have a keypad with a secret code number, which buzzes in the cabin to confirm the person trying to access the cockpit is who they say they are. Cabin crewmembers are made aware that the security door is to be opened and are taught to be on the look-out for anyone that might be acting suspiciously whilst the security door is to be opened. This forms part of the cabin crew training now and they are taught to react quickly in the event of anyone attempting to rush the door.

Despite the extensive training the crew members undergo it is not out with the realms of reasonable thinking to suggest an unarmed person could overpower the cabin crew member guarding the security door as it was about to be opened, be they male or female, and if he picked his moment perfectly may even be able to force his way into the cockpit. The timing of this act would need to be second perfect. This is not as far-fetched as one might think as the assailant would only have to get his fingers on the door edge and then the door could not be re closed and locked as the magnetic contacts need to actually touch and this would be impossible if the assailants hand or fingers were in between the door and frame. However once he had his hands on the door he would be faced with fighting two people in a confined space, namely whoever was leaving the cockpit and the steward that was manning the door on the outside. Flight crew and cabin crew are trained to deal with these kind of emergencies but there is no doubt a strong, fit, determined man could pull this off. Without being sexist I believe a woman cabin steward would offer little resistance to a strong man in this struggle, and if the member of the flight crew was caught off guard, as he surely would be, then the element of surprise might be enough to get a determined aggressive assailant into the cockpit.

Once inside the cockpit if the attacker could force the door closed, he would be fighting both pilots again in a confined space. Remember that Captain Shah on Flight MH 370 was fifty-seven years old and a fairly small slightly built man and without being rude to him would perhaps have been too weak or old to be much use in a life or death fight. The attacker in this case would probably try to kill the pilots if he had the door locked, whereas the Pilots would join the struggle, not with the intention of beating the assailant in a fight but to man handle him out of the cockpit so the door could be locked, regardless if one of the pilots was locked outside with the assailant.

If the assailant had managed to make it into the cockpit quickly, he would need to over-power the flight crew members almost immediately, as in the instance of Flight MH 370 no radio communication warning of a hijack was given. Could this be done? I think it could.

On a recent Emirates Airline flight on a Boeing 777 to Dubai shortly after take-off we were served our in flight meal, and were handed steel cutlery to use to eat with. Some airlines use plastic but on this flight it was a steel fork and knife. Now I fully accept that these aren't the world sharpest fighting implements, and would be pretty useless as slashing implements, but as stabbing implements they would kill easily. If a determined attacker wrapped the handle with the napkin provided he could easily incapacitate the person he was attacking with a hard thrust to the neck or eyeball. The attacker only has to incapacitate the crew-member and I'm sure this method will have been thought of by Jihadists. It would take perfect timing, absolute aggression and a degree of luck to successfully stab all three but there is no doubt it could be done. It is important to remember that of the four planes hijacked on September the eleventh not one of the pilots managed to call in a mayday or warning of hijack. They had insufficient time.

If we are saying a mentally unstable person, acting alone, did manage to take the plane, and that he had managed to kill or incapacitate the flight crew and lock the door and was now in control of the flight deck, alone in the cockpit, he would then have a serious problem, primarily that he would need to be able to fly the plane and would have had to have knowledge of the cockpit controls and switches. From this point I do not know if a mentally deranged person could have the calmness of mind or discipline of himself to then fly the plane in such a way as to virtually avoid the civilian radar. I am not even sure if a mentally deranged person would care about radar.

I do not think he would feel it necessary to switch off the ACARS transponder or disable the communications. If his intention was to hijack the plane and kill everyone on board, including himself, in a similar way that people who go to schools go there wanting to die by making a statement, which is enduring in its callousness and hostility, then why fly as far south, Why attempt to avoid radar? These people by and large want their names known and want the world to know they did the deed as this gives them eternal recognition, so why crash the plane where it cannot be found? Some of you may believe that this scenario should be discounted for either of these reasons.

2. Jihadist Extremist.

Planning to steal the aeroplane with the intention of landing it at a hidden airfield so it could be used in a later attack.

I am firmly of the opinion that the cockpit of virtually every aeroplane could be taken by a crew of three determined Jihadists, with the absolute exception of the Israeli Airline El Al, as they have a double safety door and this is the only system that I believe offers proper protection to the cockpit, that is why they have it. First question I would ask of this scenario is why? Why take a plane on one date, when you intend to use it on another? Surely the intelligent thing to do would be to take it at the time you intend on using it.

I know many of the families of the passengers believe this is what happened. It is the one scenario they want to be true as it allows them to believe there is a possibility of their loved ones still being alive. The reality is, however, somewhat different. Why steal a plane, then have to hide it, then have to refuel it, all the while keeping the passengers and crew imprisoned and hoping it has not been tracked, hoping that it does not get discovered by anyone, or seen by satellites. The whole time the entire flight complement needs to be fed, watered, use toilet facilities, etc, etc. I feel this is totally unreasonable.

The Jihadists win when they have control of the aeroplane in the air, and whilst it is under their control, they are in a no-lose situation, once they land they run the risk of their location being compromised and then having the plane and the passengers wrested from their control by special forces and their mission would be unsuccessful ... and why wait?

If Jihadists were planning on crashing a plane on a specific date, say, to commemorate something important to a jihad then they would hijack a plane on that date. Why do it beforehand and complicate something simple. They would never do this, and if they had, we would have definitely have heard from them before now. The specific aim of a Jihadist is to strike fear and unease by perpetrating mass murder, generally at civilian targets, as this gives them maximum effect. This is achieved, exclusively, by advertising their deeds, and keeping them secret would be utterly counterproductive.

There is however one reason I can think of that Jihadist would hijack a plane and land it, and that would be if the operation was to kidnap a special target on board. Let us look at this. Initially I felt that this was a possibility as there might have been someone on board that they needed, or that was perhaps a significant target, someone like a US Congressman or Senator, perhaps someone with a significant military background or someone from the CIA, or perhaps someone with nuclear bomb building knowledge. Even saying there was a person on board so significant that this operation was implemented; then I feel that once the aeroplane had landed and he or she had been disembarked, then the plane would have been flown into a building somewhere in a Jihadist attack.

This would serve two purposes, firstly it would be a great success as a terror weapon, and secondly it would have masked the fact that the person they were after had in fact been captured. It also fails to address the fact that the plane climbed to 45,000 feet. Why would it do this? If it did it to asphyxiate everyone on board then they would have killed their intended target of kidnap as well. It has been said that it was done to climb high above the reach of the commercial radar but any person with a computer could easily find out the position of the military radar and would very quickly be able to find out that there was plenty on the ground in the area that the aeroplane actually flew over when it turned west to cross back over the Malaysian mainland. Again you could easily verify that this system was capable of reaching beyond the 45,000 feet the plane flew at.

The aeroplane actually crossed the Malaysian peninsula very close to the Thai border so there was sure to be two sets of military radar operating in that area, so you might be able to say with some degree of confidence that the aeroplane climbing to 45,000 feet was not an anti-radar manoeuvre, as it simply did not work, and that if a group of jihadists did take the aeroplane then we would have found out before now.

Not so fast though, there is the small matter of the four Emergency Locator Transmitters, or ELTs that were on board. The locators are very robust and are made to detach themselves from the aeroplane, and float to the surface if the aeroplane crashes into water. The fact that none of these ELTs has been activated in water, or a signal received and reported acknowledging this, does tend to support the theory that the plane landed, rather than crashed. Once they are submerged they give off a signal on an emergency frequency that is picked up by satellites. These cover the entire globe. It is extremely unlikely that these transmitters would all be destroyed in the impact with the water, as they are designed to survive this. This can then only leave five possibilities as I see it;

The aeroplane did not crash on water but crashed on land and all the ELTs were destroyed on impact or did not activate as they were not submerged.

The aeroplane crashed on water and all four ELTs were destroyed on impact, which is highly improbable.

The aeroplane was in fact safely landed in a secret location.

The aeroplane crashed on water but the satellite that is meant to collect this signal and then verify the position to the emergency services was somehow temporarily disabled.

The four ELTs have been poorly serviced and their reliability unchecked, and when they were needed after the plane crashed into the water simply did not work.

Let us look at these possibilities. There is a real chance that the aeroplane has crashed on a remote piece of land and has gone undiscovered. The fact is that the search crews have been looking exclusively in the Southern and

Indian Oceans since the Inmarsat Satellite data was released, and there are many jungle areas in both Malaysia and Indonesia that this aeroplane could have crashed into without any chance of finding them, especially as no one is actually looking for the plane on land. The ELTs are designed to be jettisoned if the aeroplane senses it is about to crash, however if the plane sensed that it was being landed as opposed to crashed, and the flight computer does this with a combination of data from the altimeter and onboard radar, even on water, they would not be jettisoned and may have gone down with a rapidly sinking aeroplane.

Safely landed in a secret location ... cannot think of one reason why. There is no doubt that the CIA has the ability to temporarily, or even permanently, disable the satellite responsible for collecting the emergency signal and passing on the location to the emergency services. Almost unbelievably the ELTs on Flight MH 370 have NO record of having been serviced or of having new batteries fitted at any time in its life.

3. The CIA

The CIA stole the plane to stage a terrorist incident and thus continue the fear mongering amongst the American people with the intention of allowing them to further erode peoples' civil liberties and to help them persuade congress and the Senate that eavesdropping around the world and in the US is a necessary infringement on peoples' privacy and civil freedom as it is a vital tool in the war on terror.

As far as I am concerned the US Government would never sanction an operation like this, as it could and in fact probably would lead to a war with China as 153 of their innocent civilians would have been basically executed by the CIA, and for sure the Chinese, or anyone else from any country could not allow that to go unpunished. Now don't get me wrong the CIA has done some incredibly horrendous stuff over the years to innocent people in the name of freedom, and we can quote 'Agent Orange' as a prime example. They have been shown constantly down through the years to lack any respect for human life and have often lacked self-control, as most self-governing bodies do; but there is no way this happened. Yes the flight did fall of the Flightradar24 online live tracker a minute or so after take-off and the apparent vanishing act does look very suspicious, and indeed something of this order would need an organisation like the CIA to pull it off ... but why would they?

If they wanted to have a plane crashed into a building to keep everyone in a state of fear then they wouldn't have to pretend to steal it and cover it up, that would be ridiculously complicated. They would just allow actual jihadists to do it by dropping them off the no fly lists and with a little double-agent trickery thrown, pretend they knew nothing about it. This would give them perfect deniability for the deed. I think I can say with some certainty that the CIA is not this out of control. They would need a very substantial reason to become involved in something like this.

So on and so forth, all other possibilities are really unlikely or are just idiotic, or just don't fit all the facts.

So what really happened?

Here is another version, make your own mind up if you think it is possible.

Either a member of the flight crew – perhaps one alone, or both acting together – or a passenger or passengers either acting with or independently of the flight crew, took control of the plane.

The flight was taken not for political reasons but religious reasons. The flight was taken by an Islamic fundamentalist or fundamentalists for a jihad mission to kill Americans.

There is no doubt it would be a relatively simple task for either of the flight crew to achieve this, both were Muslim, and both were in a position where they could relatively easily lock the other out of the cockpit and assume control of the aeroplane. There is actually no one demographic for a jihadist, when Glasgow airport was attacked the attackers were doctors, surgeons and consultants. Some are wealthy, Bin Laden himself came from an extremely wealthy family, his father was a billionaire and was finally shot and killed in a large house in an upperclass residential area of Islamabad in Pakistan –some are poor, some are educated, some are less so. Some have suffered family loss at the hands of the war on terror, and some have not – as I say there is no specific blueprint for someone to become an Islamic extremist, so we cannot discount either of the pilots being responsible simply because they are pilots. Point of fact is that the people who radicalise people to the more extreme version of Islam have been ordered by the Al Qaeda leadership to specifically try to target commercial passenger aeroplane pilots for radicalisation for years, as this would precluded the need to hijack the cockpit, which is a difficult and risky part of a hijack operation. The fact that both the pilots had family is not to be considered a viable reason to exclude them from being possible Jihadists, as many suicide bombers are in fact seemingly happily married with children. One of the bombers that blew up the trains and buses in London had been recently married, had a newborn baby and was apparently a good husband and father.

The act of taking the flight alone by one of the flight crew is as simple as waiting for the other flight crew member to go to the toilet, which is in the forward galley area, and as it was a late night flight there is every chance that both would have been drinking coffee to help them stay awake, and would have possibly needed a comfort break. There is an international rule that states the pilots are not to be disturbed during the first half an hour of a flight and it could be that one of the flight crew suggested to the other that he use the toilet first once this period was over. Once his counterpart had left, he relocked the door, to put his plan into action. The first thing that had to be done, the ACARS flight transponder would be switched off. Whoever had gained control, captain or vice captain would then have to say a cursory sign off to the Malaysian Air Traffic Control, and then deactivate the in-flight mobile phone communications and in-flight cockpit communications. That would be phase one of the hijack complete. It would have taken a few seconds. The member of the flight crew that had left to use the toilet would then return to find he was locked out of the cockpit and there was no response from the intercom phone.

No doubt the alarm would be raised amongst the passengers once the member of the flight crew realised he had been locked out but what could they do … well quite a lot actually … it may surprise or even amaze everyone to hear this but the cockpit steel door is in fact bypassable.

Under normal circumstances if a crew member is locked out on a flight today the protocol for opening the door goes like this; the satellite phone would be used to contact the engineers for Malaysian Airlines on the ground and they can send a signal through the flight control communications to release the door mechanism. The senior flight attendant would have a series of special codewords and numbers she would need to give in the correct sequence to verify firstly, who she is, and that she is who she says she is, and that this was a request that was given WITHOUT being under duress. There would be a specific code word that would be given by her in the event of there being a threat to the flight or to her person, which would warn the engineer on the ground as to what was happening. You should however feel reassured that there is virtually no way a steward would compromise this safety feature as they all know that a terrorist taking the cockpit would likely spell death for them anyway.

The situation on Flight MH 370 was different however, as the communications had been switched off and no mobile phone towers were anyway near close enough to allow mobile phones to be useful, this would leave the cabin crew locked out and unable to call the engineer. Now you might think that that would be that and there was no hope of opening the door, but you would be wrong. I mentioned earlier the security door is sealed with electromagnetic locks, which are powered by 6 volt electricity – the fuse for which is located under the cockpit itself in the forward engineering compartment. This can be accessed by the hatch in the floor in the forward galley on all Boeing 777s. This is a simple job of opening the hatch and climbing down the steel fixed ladder. The forward engineering bay is forwards of the ladder bottom and the large fuse boards are located in here. The correct fuse would then need to be identified and the breaker switched off. Once the breaker has been tripped the locks are automatically disabled and the door would be unlocked. Whoever it was that was locked out of the cockpit would climb back out of the hatch in the forward galley and with the enlisted help of the passengers and other crew-members attempt to re-take the cockpit by force.

As I stated before it is an outward opening door so only a couple of people could pull on it at a time, and the hijacker, whichever it was may have had enough sense to bring along a length of rope in his carry-on luggage or even around his waist so he could tie the door off inside the cockpit. Either way, I believe his next course of action was indicative of someone attempting to repel a cockpit attack. One of the things that always perplexed me about this incident was why did the flight climb to 45,000 feet immediately after the hijack? I think I may have the answer.

Immediately after the September 11 attacks on America, the aviation industry was in an extremely compromised position. The terrorists on that day had exposed a gaping hole in aviation security, which had in turn exposed an even more enormous hole in America's strategic defences. There was still the same enormous demand for passenger flights and to allow flying to continue around the globe the various Governments, security experts and the leaders from the aviation industry had to come up with a short-term solution to the obvious problem of flights being hijacked and then being turned into human guided terror missiles. This was the interim measure they implemented. This was before the steel cockpit doors were retrofitted to passenger aeroplanes.

The pilots were instructed that in the event of someone trying to gain forcible access to the cockpit that they should be engaged in hand-to-hand combat immediately by all members of the cabin crew and the flight crew, with the exception of whoever was piloting the plane. They were to remain seated and to put the plane into a high speed and as near vertical as possible, rapid climb. This was done in an attempt to allow gravity and the acceleration G-Force to help the copilot that was not flying the aeroplane – basically the one doing the fighting – to defeat the assailants trying to force their way into the cockpit. As the plane climbs the pilot fighting was trained to use his weight to force them out of the cockpit enough so the door could be kicked shut, whereby it would lock automatically albeit on a fairly flimsy lock. The cabin crew were trained to if necessary, enlist help from the passengers to defeat the assailants with weight of numbers and subdue them en-mass. Once they were subdued they would be manacled to their seats, all f lights now have these handcuffs on board as part of the safety equipment. If it looked to the pilot that control could not be established he would put the flight into a parabolic dive. This is done by NASA Astronauts as a way of training them for weightlessness and basically uses the rapidly falling plane to help defeat the assailants by making them and everyone else on board weightless and thus disrupting their attack. This is done with the copilot constantly urging the passengers to get involved to save themselves, as the attack would probably turn out to mean death for everyone on board if it succeeded.

This parabolic flight pattern would prove extremely difficult for any assailant to overcome, but it does come with certain risks for the aeroplane itself. You see passenger aeroplanes are not built to take the enormous stresses this kind of flying puts on the aeroplane structure and there is a very real chance of stress rupturing the aeroplane and tearing it apart. It is a fine line. I wondered if the climb to 45,000 feet that MH 370 did was indicative of a pilot trying to fend off a cockpit attack, but when I asked commercial airline pilots that very question I was amazed at the response.

Many pilots I have spoken to have said that if they were on a flight and there was a serious attack on the cockpit they would indeed immediately instigate a rapid climb, and that they would switch the cabin pressurisation switches from 'auto' to 'manual' immediately and use altitude hypoxia to either kill or at least incapacitate the assailants. Many believe the sudden depressurisation and subsequent emergency oxygen mask deployment would panic the attackers also and thus further disrupt their attack, this has never been a recognised method of repelling an attack, but it seems to be one many pilots have secretly adopted themselves.

Once the plane has reached 45,000 feet hypoxia would quickly overtake the perpetrators, and anyone else not wearing their oxygen mask or one of the pressurised oxygen masks the crew have in the lockers. The drop down emergency masks work off an oxygen generator and are completely depleted after ten short minutes, the bottled cylinder the crew use can last fifteen to twenty minutes if they breath shallow, less if they are gulping air. At 45,000 feet the air is so thin and the pressure so low that breathe is effectively sucked from your lungs and unconsciousness would arrive in thirty seconds or so, with death within a couple of minutes.

It would be possible for the copilot that had been doing the fighting, if he had managed to put on his pressurised cylinder, to wait until this asphyxiation was under way and to use this moment to handcuff the assailants, whereby the pilot flying would be given the all clear to return the cabin pressurisation switch back to auto and he would put the plane in a dive to a lower altitude, usually 12,000 feet. Passengers would be able to regain consciousness by breathing the cabin air. This looks very similar to the kind of altitude alterations this flight took, however the length of time spent at the 45,000 feet, more than twenty minutes, would have killed everyone on board not wearing a pressurised cylinder replacement air mask, and in fact even the cylinder masks would have depleted by then. According to the Malaysian Military radar immediately after the flight signed off from Malaysian Air Traffic Control the flight turned west and climbed to 45,000 feet. It remained there for some twenty-one minutes, and then dropped rapidly to 12,000 feet.

If you believe that this scenario is what happened to MH370, then whoever took the plane, and it is impossible to establish with the facts we have to date who that person is, or persons are, may have switched the cabin pressure switch from automatic to manual. This would have resulted in the cabin depressurising, the replacement air masks would deploy … thus occupying the cabin crew and even the other member of the flight crew that had been locked out of the cockpit, as they would have to scramble for their own pressurised masks and then spend valuable minutes helping the passengers on with theirs. All the while climbing the plane into the deadly heights where all the hijacker would have to do is wait whilst everyone on board died of asphyxiation, basically murdered by suffocation. He would have access to two pressurised cylinders in the cockpit, his own and the other member of the flight crews, and would then only have to wait 15 to 20 minutes till all the remaining crews cylinder masks were depleted and everyone else on board was murdered by his hand, thus he would have full control of the flight to do with as he pleased.

It may be that with this scenario we have explained why the aeroplane climbed to 45,000 feet that night, for surely that was not done without a good reason. The flight crew hijacker could then dive the plane to 12,000 feet and this is perhaps significant; as pilots are trained to drop the plane quickly to 12,000 feet in the event of a decompression event, as the air is sufficiently oxygenated to allow a human to breathe at this altitude, and pilots would train in the flight simulators to do this every time they had their masks on.

It may well be that if the plane was taken by one of the Pilots that this was a case of muscle memory and whichever one it was descending to 12,000 feet as a trained reaction. After this the plane was dropped down even lower to 5,000 feet as shown by both Malaysian and Thai military radar. This has all the hallmarks of someone trying to evade radar, in fact some sources have suggested the plane dropped significantly lower – all this was done – the reason the flight was tracked north by the military radar was simple. The pilot would be fairly aware where the civilian radar beacons were and was trying to avoid them, but had underestimated in his planning the strength of the military radar positions.

Phase one of the plan to take the plane would seem very simple but there is perhaps a problem. This entire case of the missing aeroplane is deciphered by timing. You see the timing required to have the other member of the flight crew out of the cockpit at exactly the correct time by asking him to go to the toilet seems a bit weak to me. I think a more sinister event befell the innocent flight crew member. I think for the timing to be so perfect, so that the aeroplane could sign off from the Malaysian Air Traffic Control and then immediately turn west has to mean that the non-Jihadist pilot was incapacitated or murdered in the cockpit some time shortly before the final hand off to the Malaysian Air Traffic Control.

I think that would be the only way that the Jihadist pilot could ensure he could do the hand off to the Malaysian Air Traffic Control and turn immediately without any possibility of the non-Jihadist pilot raising the alarm on the satellite phone, which would be still operational until after the final hand off to the Malaysian Air Traffic Control. And what if the non-Jihadist pilot declined the offer of a toilet break? The plan would have been ruined, and there is no way a committed Jihadist would allow sympathy to any one person to compromise his operation. If I was planning this mission I would probably have either drugged the other pilot or poisoned him, or even simply pretended to check something in the fuseboard behind him, and approach him silently from behind and strangled him. Either of these solutions would allow the perfect timing of the hijack.

Phase two would then be very simple, a climb into the deadly heights and he could ensure his plan would not be interrupted by the passengers and crew storming the cockpit, by murdering every single one of them, man, woman and child by asphyxiation.

Phase three would mean a serious loss of altitude, initially down to 12,000 feet so he could remove his replacement air mask, and after a short period there down to 5,000 feet as all that was left to do was to evade radar so as to not alert anyone that the plane had been hijacked, and this was done by flying up the Andaman Sea before another west turn, and then finally to turn the plane to the direction of his primary objective which was Diego Garcia, so he could use the aeroplane as a human guided missile just as the Jihadists had done on the September Eleventh attacks.

Phase four would be a simple case of setting the navigation computer to navigate a course to the final destination of Diego Garcia, whilst maintaining a height of probably 4,000 to 5,000 feet, and then waiting. In this instance the hijacker had failed to note the position or capabilities of the Malaysian or Thai Military radars, and he had no way of knowing about Americas advanced satellite capabilities, and this would cost him his Jihad. His life was already lost and would end that night one way or another, but his Jihad would fail.

I believe that the American Government have covered up this tragedy for a number of reasons but the main reason is if they admitted shooting down this aeroplane they would almost definitely have to admit they have this satellite tracking capability, and they want that kept secret, at any cost. The aeroplane would have been intercepted by a US Military fighter and once international protocols (which I will deal with later in this book) and Presidential authorisation had been obtained, the flight would have been shot out of the sky.

There is quite a bit of compelling evidence to suggest one of the pilots took the flight alone and not whilst acting with the other pilot. Put very simply, I feel sure that if someone had managed to radicalise two pilots, then I feel sure they would have taken the opportunity to take two planes, one each, and not one between them. Surely two pilots committed to the Jihad would mean two aeroplanes taken in this way and not one.

Remember it was late at night. One in the morning when the flight ACARS was switched off, so any Jihadist looking to kill Americans would not have the luxury of killing them by crashing into an American Embassy somewhere in the Far East, as they would all be virtually deserted save for cleaners, which are usually locals, and some security. If, as I suspect, the target was to kill as many Americans as possible, then the only place that could guarantee a large number of American Military and CIA personnel was the airbase at Diego Garcia.

The idea put into everyone's head that this was perhaps not a jihadist motivated attack rather than a hijack for political reasons was foisted into our thinking on the very first day ... and again timing shows us the truth.

The Malaysian Government said on 8 March that 'this was not a terrorist motivated incident.' They said this without having had any time at all to check properly if that was the case. I have my suspicions that they already knew the flight was a Jihadist hijack but had agreed with the Americans to stay silent about this fact and then they seized on this opportunity to besmirch the good name of Captain Shah, whether he was guilty or not, specifically as he was a relation of the political opposition and a passionate supporter of his relatives politics.

The Malaysian Government hoped to tie Captain Shah to this flight disappearance as a suicide/ mass murder and hoped to gain politically from this by painting the opposition Party as 'aggressive zealots'. I firmly believe anyone motivated so strongly by Malaysian politics that they would hijack an aeroplane, would have in the worst case scenario crashed the plane into an opposition political party target in Kuala Lumpur, or even the Parliament Buildings there, or more likely to have landed the aeroplane back in Kuala Lumpur having raised awareness to his political situation. People of a political determined persuasion want to influence people to vote with them, and not to alienate them by aggressive acts. None of which happened in this case, and if anything, flying the aeroplane to a remote location and killing everyone on board would be utterly counterproductive.

You see the timing IS critical once again, the Malaysian Government must have known what had happened to Flight MH 370 that first day, as they were happily allowing everyone to believe it was Captain Shah's fault by drip-feeding all the nonsense about him; that he was mentally unstable, and that he was recently separated from his wife, and that his political mentor had been jailed that day, and that he had a flight simulator at home, and that he had become withdrawn, etc, etc ,etc – all of this they fed to the press in an underhand manner to besmirch his good name, but they forgot one thing – it was the copilot Fariq Abdul Hamid's voice that was on the recording of the final transmission from the flight to Malaysian Air Traffic Control, and Minister Hussein would have known this.

This explains why he gave the wrong information to the media the day he was asked about it ... when he said the last words were 'Alright, goodnight' instead of 'Good night, Malaysian 370' ... because in that second that he was asked that unexpected question he realised the voice on the tape, once analysed by the FBI would betray their lies, and he flapped, big time. From the moment he gave the incorrect answer to that question Minister Hussein has looked like a man slowly being walked to the gallows.

All the facts, taken as a whole, point to this being a terrorist attack. Terrorists tend to keep their attacks silent until the actual terror incident happens. In this case the plane looks to have been flown in a way consistent with someone trying to avoid radar. Just like the Jihad pilots did on September the Eleventh. If this was a suicide/murder then why try and conceal your position, why would he care? The actual act of hijack being kept as covert as possible by the Jihadists, until the ultimate target was announced by crashing into them. This looks exactly like what happened here. It looks like the Jihadist had chosen a military target, and specifically one that has been used extensively during military operations in the Middle East, maybe Diego Garcia was chosen because it was the only place within the range of the aircraft that could guarantee large numbers of American personnel at that time of day.

Whatever the reason, the Flight MH 370 definitely went there, because there are independent witnesses that saw it on route – lots of them in fact. The Island of Kuda Huvadhoo is one of many coral islands that make up the Maldives, and on the morning of 8 March many of the residents of this Island were awoken by a large passenger jet, flying very low over the Islands. The plane was described as a large passenger jet airliner, white in colour with a red stripe – exactly like the colour decals on a Malaysian Airliner. Furthermore it was over the Island at 06.15 Malaysian time and that is within the time frame of how long it would take to cover the distance flown from the last known point of contact if the plane was flying relatively slowly, as it would be if it had flown there as suspected at low altitude. The plane was also on a bearing flying from the north to the southeast, which is the perfect bearing to take it to Diego Garcia and the final piece of evidence is; the final bearing that the military radar from the Thai and Malaysian Military show the plane to be flying on has it flying directly to the Maldives. You probably will not believe that the Malaysian Government spokesperson, Minister Hussein categorically dismissed this as being Flight MH 370 from the outset and they never even sent anyone to ask questions, or show the witnesses pictures of the planes to see if they could properly identify the Malaysian Airlines colour decals. There is no way they would do that if they were properly looking for a missing aeroplane ... zero chance.

Now some of you may be sceptical that this is all true, so I will attempt to prove it beyond any reasonable doubt. You see I can quote the Internet website FlightTracker24 as proof. They have, as I have said before, an enormous data-base of commercial flights stretching back years, and they do not have one flight in their data-base over-flying the Island of Kuda Huvadhoo at that time on 8 March, so either the locals got together in a mass, hysterical, group lie, or it was, what we think it is, and it was the pilot on his way to attack the base at Diego Garcia –I am pretty sure I know which I believe.

Of the two pilots on board that night there is no doubt that one looks a more likely candidate than the other. In fact, most people seem to have Captain Shah convicted already and perhaps there is some merit in this, and once you look at all the facts, and if you believe what the Malaysian Government say about him, then many do in fact point to him, however not all. There is one huge fact that no one can deny actually just about proves his innocence, namely the fact that it was the copilot Fariq Hamid that spoke to Malaysian Air Traffic Control when the final communication was being given and NOT Captain Shah.

In the search for fairness though, we will explore the evidence showing if either pilot could have been involved in the disappearance of the flight. In the months before the incident of the Malaysian Flight MH 370 going missing Captain Shah had, by the admission of his family, changed as a person. His personality had changed, and he had changed emotionally and this had led to him becoming separated from his wife of 30 years, without any other party being involved. They were set to be divorced, a huge emotional upheaval in any person's life. He had become distanced from the other members of his family, two sons and a daughter, which was a particularly strange occurrence as he had always been described as a family man. He had fallen out with old friends, and had become politically aggressive.

His political mentor, the leader of the opposition to the long term Government, had been jailed for five years for sodomy on 7 March, the day before flight MH 370 had gone missing, and Captain Shah had attended the trial. Captain Shah had admitted to being in a mental state of 'utter frustration' at the charges and subsequent conviction of the opposition leader on what were widely regarded throughout Malaysia as trumped up charges put in place by the ruling Government. Captain Shah's wife had admitted that in the months prior to Flight MH 370 going missing, whilst they were still living together, he had become distant, and would retreat to spend long hours alone in front of his computer and flight simulator. He had hardly even spoke to his sons during that period, which was particularly unusual for him, as he had always been a good father and had maintained good communications with his children throughout their lives – many surviving members of families who have had a family member radicalised have a similar tale to tell.

However there is one glaring fact that once again, whilst being linked to the timing of the events might be sufficient to exonerate Captain Shah. You see the final communication to Malaysian Air Traffic Control which said 'Goodnight, Malaysian 370' was analysed by the Malaysian authorities and the FBI in America, and they stated it was the voice of the flight vice captain, 27-year-old Abdul Fariq. Now if we consider as fact that the ACARS transponder had been switched off prior to this last communication it would look more like the copilot was to blame for the flight hijack and not the captain that was involved. There is one problem however and it is the fact that we cannot say with any degree of accuracy when the transponder was switched off, or even if it was switched off before the communications were as these are designed to reply to a radar message every half hour or so and only twelve minutes had passed from the previous ACARS message, so it was not due to update the ACARS for another eighteen minutes. It could well be that the ACARS transponder was switched off after the final communication.

The fact that Captain Shah had been acting out of character has no doubt cast suspicion on him, and many believe that this would support, almost absolutely, the case to prove his involvement. All we can say for sure is that there is in fact a certain amount of evidence to suggest either might be involved and enough to support that neither is. You will have to make up your own mind on this.

4. Jihadist extremist using advanced computer hacking hijacked the plane to attack American military base of Diego Garcia.

It has long been thought of as a possibility amongst some computer hackers that if they really put their minds to it that they could use the uplink for the on-board wifi connection that many aeroplanes have now, to hack into the aeroplanes onboard navigation computer, and mainframe computer to effectively fly the aeroplane from a computer on the ground, against the will of whoever was piloting the aeroplane. This may sound fanciful but once you discuss this with a bona-fide hacker it is in fact something they feel they can do, frighteningly easily. Most average holiday package tour passengers are unaware of the fact that modern commercial airliners are mostly flown by onboard computers and seldom by the onboard Pilots.

Before the aeroplane takes off all of the relevant flight details are loaded into the navigation computer by the pilots, this will include all navigational turns and waypoints the aeroplane must make, altitudes, speed, and final destination, including the runway the aeroplane is to land on. Once these are loaded into the navigation computer and the aeroplane has taken off, if the pilots then chose to do so, then both pilots could effectively jump out of the aeroplane on parachutes, and so long as they had engaged the navigational computer – or autopilot as most of you will know it – then the computer itself would carry on flying the aeroplane to its final destination, where it would land the aeroplane on the correct runway.

Point of fact; the systems are so advanced now that the human is fast becoming the weak point in the loop. Pilots do not actually land the aeroplanes, computers do, and the pilots now are, generally speaking, as much a passenger during that phase of the flight as the paying punters in the passenger areas. Many airlines now are looking at flying passenger aeroplanes in the same way that the autonomous flying drones do. These are not like remotely piloted drones as there is no human live flying them, the entire details of the flight are pre-programmed into the drones flight computer and it flies a preset route for a preset time at preset altitudes and speed, and once it has completed its task it flies back to a preset runway and lands itself. Now the system at the moment is not one that is built to be operated in this manner; however all of the pieces of hardware are in place so that if someone with great hacking ability could access it mid-flight they all agree it could be done. The fairly recent advent of onboard wifi, is perfect for a hacker to find a way into the aeroplanes computer. I do not confess to have anything like the capabilities of computer hackers but I am wise enough to realise if you give someone the ability to access any computer, then a good hacker can eventually work out a way to control it, against your will.

The 2002 electrical blackouts in America were done by computer hackers who were able to infiltrate the computer systems of the electrical grid company and subsequently caused chaos. The eventual monetary cost was put in the hundreds of billions of dollars. The system was supposed to be fully protected by the most up-to-date firewall and isolated from any kind of remote connection, yet the hackers still found a way in.

Now this is going to scare a few people; every year there is a cyber security hacking conference held. During this conference, cyber security experts from all over the world meet up to discuss the latest cyber hacking trends and offer their solutions to these problems. In 2013 at this very conference a well known industry security analyst stood on stage and switched on his mobile phone and booted up an 'App' which he had coded himself, this App has become famous throughout the cyber security industry, it is called 'Planespoilt'. With this App the operator has the ability to remotely download false data into two key technological pieces of the aeroplanes cockpit, namely the Automatic Dependent Surveillance-Broadcast (ADS-B), which talks to Air Traffic Controllers, and the Aircraft Communications Addressing and Reporting System (ACARS) which controls communications between aeroplanes, this data and remote information manipulation could fool the pilots in the cockpit into believing the false data and allow the 'Planespoilt App' user to remotely control the aeroplane from a seat in the passenger area.

This technology is fairly new, but I am sure it could be refined to create a situation where the pilots are left unable to command the aeroplane. So if we assume that the hacking ability does now exist and is advanced enough that an aeroplane could be hijacked mid- flight in this way, let us see if the facts we know can fit this theory.

My fairly rudimental knowledge of hacking, and a complete distrust of anything computer orientated often makes me believe that computer hackers can do just about anything they want with impunity. Apart from a few over-intelligent, but equally over stupid hackers, who have attacked the US Military and attempted to hack into the launch codes for nuclear ballistic missiles and have been jailed, no one seems to go to jail for hacking. The UK Government is apparently defending itself from a million attempted computer hacks per day, and for the life of me I cannot remember the last time someone was charged in this country for that crime. This complete lack of policing of computer hacking has bred a generation of hackers around the world that are emboldened to do as they please, and seem to revel in the fact that they can act without any fear of being taken to court. As a result the scale of the computer attacks that they are now involved in has escalated enormously. There is a worldwide ego contest between these hackers to see who can achieve the most dramatic, or devastating, or newsworthy hack, so they can assume the position of 'world's best hacker'.

> One of the problems with this theory that I have found straight away is that whilst I have no doubt that an aeroplane could be hacked, simply because it has a wifi up-link to it, and history has

shown us many times, that if there is a way of speaking to a computer, then it can be hacked – without exception. However the communications to this aeroplane were cut immediately, which would sever the up-link connection.

Now as part of the safety procedures on board a passenger aeroplane I know that an engineer from the ground can remotely open the cockpit security door by sending a message through the wifi up-link to the computer. This is a recent security upgrade in case both pilots are incapacitated inside the cockpit and the cabin crew need to get in, or if one of the pilots locks the other out and is intent on committing suicide by crashing the aeroplane. These two scenarios have both happened before and this was the finding of the Air Accident Enquiry, which suggested the extra measure of remote door opening. Now if there is a way that ground engineers can access the main computer, then that system could be hacked, no sweat. Then we could have a position of jihadists or other persons willing to attack the cockpit, if they were perfectly co-ordinated with the ground hacker, being able to simply walk through the cockpit security door, just as was done on September the Eleventh and then murder the flight crew and assume control of the cockpit. The hacker would then be able to lock the door behind them. The computer hacker on the ground or the jihadists in the cockpit could then fly the aeroplane wherever they wanted.

This is a very feasible option in my mind, but there is no doubt that a lone jihadist would find it extremely difficult to take the aircraft as I outlined earlier when I discussed the possibility of a deranged person taking the cockpit. However, I think two or three trained, fit, determined Jihadists, acting together in a strategically concerted attack, could in fact, quite easily take control of the cockpit ... whether they could do this before the pilot raised the alarm over the radio is something I will discuss later, but for my money they could. It is worthy of mention at this time that only one of the pilots that were in the cockpits that were attacked and taken by the Jihadists on September the Eleventh attacks, managed to raise the alarm, so it may in fact not be that big of a surprise.

Now many of you would believe that a combined effort to rush the security door at the cockpit would be the preferred choice of jihadists, but that would be extremely difficult timing wise, and if they failed in their attempt they are locked out by the security door and the pilots have control, and their mission is defeated before it has really started. They would then no doubt be left at the mercy of the rest of the passengers, and I know how I would react in that situation, they would do well to survive the flight to the nearest airport, and even if they did, they are then faced with the prospect of the remainder of their lives spent in solitary confinement in jail. I think the attempt to rush the door has too little chance of success, and for that reason I do not think it would be attempted.

> I also believe there would be another way for jihadists or other determined and organised

people to take the cockpit by defeating the security door, so let us explore the other possibilities. On the Boeing 777 at the front galley there is a hatch in the floor, which leads to the sub floor area, it is there on all Boeing 777s. Once the hatch has been lifted this exposes a ladder which leads down to the area under the galley. Ahead of this towards the front of the aeroplane there is the forward engineering room, it is only five or six paces forward, and there is no security door – this houses some of the on-board computers, various flight control equipment and the master fuse board. Located in here is the circuit breaker for the door locking mechanism, they are magnetic and use 6 volt electricity to operate the magnets that lock the door. If this breaker could be accessed and switched off then no power equals no lock. Now if the pilots realise this is happening before the attack on the cockpit then pilots are far from a sitting duck, as they could probably adequately defend the cockpit using the parabolic flight to altitude and hypoxia as a defence, which we outlined earlier. The problem with the parabolic flight defence in this instance being that even if the copilot managed to fight the attackers out the door, and I think because he would have gravity and G-force to help him, he would, then the pilot left flying the aeroplane could not lock the door once they were outside as the electricity had been cut. This would mean an ongoing fight between the pilot that was fighting and the assailants and I think the Jihadists would win in quick time, especially if they armed themselves with the metal knives they now seem happy to give you on flights. During this kind of attempt on the cockpit the pilot flying would probably have had time to call out an emergency and as that never happened we must look elsewhere for another solution.

It would undoubtedly be advantageous to the attackers if the circuit breaker for the security door could be switched off, without the cabin crew or the flight crew either noticing or having time to react. Is it possible that this could this be done? Is it at all feasible that someone could go down the hatch without being seen? I have regularly witnessed an empty forward galley on these planes myself – sometimes for an extended period of time. To access the hatch, and climb down the ladder, and then replace the hatch above you, would only take a few seconds if it was practiced, and as it was a night flight the cabin lights would be dimmed at this point in the flight, so the ambient light would not carry into this area, although it is lit itself. The majority of passengers would be watching a movie with their headphones on and would probably not notice, and the others might be reading a book or sleeping, and their distracted attention would no doubt further help any potential attackers.

So it is not outside the realms of the possible that a well trained couple of attackers could get up from their seats once the cabin lights had been dimmed and make like they are going to the forward toilet. They would strategically wait until the forward galley is completely empty, a common occurrence. One member of the team lifts the cover hatch and the second member jumps down. The first member then replaces the hatch and walks on to the toilet door. The forward galley area is screened from the passengers' seats anyway so I think this could be done no problem.

There, outside the toilet door the jihadist is joined by the third member of the assault team, whilst they wait for the signal from the member of their team in the subfloor area confirming that the security has been de-activated. The member in the subfloor area pulls the fuse for the ACARS transponder, the communications and the security door and then signals to his friends to attack. He then does not, as you might assume, make his way out to assist them in their attack. He waits down below, and in turn, listens for a signal that would tell him they were in the cockpit; it would only take a few short seconds, five at the most. Once he hears the signal he would replace the fuse in the door lock, and lock the two assailants and the two pilots in the cockpit. The pilots, who would have been oblivious of this attack until the two assailants came through the security door, just to their rear, brandishing the cutlery knife they had been given with their meal, or that they had collected on their way through the forward galley. The pilot and co pilot would be seated and generally speaking seat belted into their seats and would be absolutely unable to defend themselves. Crucial to the scenario we are dealing with on flight MH 370, unable to raise the alarm, as they would be pitched immediately into a fight for their lives.

Even if the communications breaker was not switched off there would have been no time to raise the alarm – if the jihadists then gained control of the cockpit, and I can see no way the two Pilots could have defended themselves from two assailants armed with steel knives, then the Jihadists would be in absolute control but would be faced with a series of problems.

If the member of the team that climbed down into the sub-floor area, did not throw the breaker switch for the security door back on but instead rushed back up the steps through the hatch to join the assault on the cockpit then the lock on the door would now be disabled and the cabin crew and passengers would no doubt react aggressively, as I would in that situation, and the Jihadists would be open to a similar attack on the cockpit from the passengers, as they had just mounted themselves.

The main difference being that they would find themselves under attack from many dozens of people, realising their lives depended on regaining control of the aeroplane, and there would be little hope of them wining that battle. This has been done before on September the Eleventh attacks and the Jihadists on that day, realising they were about to lose the flight deck themselves, simply crashed the aeroplane into the ground, and whilst they failed in their ultimate goal which was to attack the Whitehouse, they still managed to spread utter terror which was the actual point of the whole thing.

As no wreckage has been found near the point that the aeroplane was taken from then I think that it is safe to assume that the terrorist that accessed the sub-floor area would have waited there, and then re-activated the door once the two man attack team had entered the cockpit. He would undoubtedly be consigning himself to death for his action, for if he resurfaced through the hatch he would be set upon by the passengers, who would be oblivious as to how to disable the security door, and would probably just beat him to death, or if he remained down below in the sub-floor area he would be killed alongside everyone else on board, with the exception of the two Jihadists, of asphyxiation. History has shown that in all probability he would not be too bothered either way, as he was sure to die anyway, and the object of a Jihad is to lay down your life whilst defeating the enemies of Islam.

Make no mistake this is very feasible, and it is perhaps surprising, that it has not happened before now. All it would take is correct planning and execution by a sufficiently organised, trained, ruthless and committed three-man team. These are skills many jihadists have shown in the past. As a point of fact only one pilot in the September Eleven attacks was able to raise the alarm when the cockpits were rushed. This attack would really only require the first terrorist to successfully access the hatch in the forward galley undetected, and then the storming of the cock pit is an extremely easy task, a virtual carbon copy of the 9/11 attacks. So history has proven this to be possible, and in fact, if the security door electrical supply was manipulated as I have suggested, then it would actually be the perfect tool to protect the attackers.

Once the two man attack team were locked inside the cockpit, and both pilots were incapacitated, probably as I have suggested by stabbing, or even hand to hand combat, and control had been established by the jihadists, one of them could then assume their position at the controls of the aeroplane, whilst the other guarded the door. I feel the radar evidence shows that they then initiated their own high speed and steep climb to 45,000ft, and the only explanation for that would be, so they could combine the altitude with switching the cabin pressurisation switch from auto to manual, in order to murder the passengers. This horrendously callous deed would leave their fellow jihadist dead also, but this would ensure they were fully secure, and in control of the aircraft without the possibility of anyone re-taking the flight from them. Then they could fully concentrate on the next part of their Jihad mission, which was to kill Americans by attacking the Island of Diego Garcia.

They would have to drop the aeroplane down to 12,000 feet to stabilise the cabin air to a safe to breathable level, before their own emergency replacement air supply ran out. Once down at 12,000 feet they would switch the cabin pressurisation switch back to auto, as a safety precaution, in case they had to climb the aeroplane again, and then set their altitude even lower, down to

5,000 feet or even lower as the military radar has indicated, to help avoid radar detection, which would alert authorities to the hijack. This was important to the Jihadists as an aeroplane that was suspected of being hijacked would have fighter jets from any nearby capable military speeding to intercept them, and this would ruin their chances of attacking Diego Garcia.

A direction would be plotted north, up the middle of the Andaman Sea to also avoid the commercial radar and then west once well clear of Indonesian radar and finally southwest, but critically not directly to Diego Garcia, but directly to the Maldives, the flight heading directly to the Maldives would help them hide their intentions should their position be compromised by shipborne radar along the way. Once the Jihadists reached the Maldives they would turn southeast, in this case over an Island called Kuda Huvadhoo, flying low and as fast as they could, the jet engines noise signature being so loud it actually woke the local people in their beds. Remember, the timing once again, shows us that the flight would have arrived at Kuda Huvadhoo at pretty much the correct time the locals said it did, specifically 06.15 Malaysian time, but this was 03.15 in the morning local time on Kuda Huvadhoo. The noise must have been very significant to get people awake and out of their beds, which is very suggestive of a low flying powerful jet. Once again timing shows us the truth.

The terrorists that attacked the twin towers flew low over America and Manhattan Island; contour mapping in military parlance, in an effort to avoid radar detection ... as was done in this case.

The authorities in Malaysia have been at pains to reiterate, that background checks on the passengers has failed to identify one person with actual links to any kind of radicalised cleric or terrorist movement, let alone three, the two Iranian passengers definitely spring to mind here, and as they are still an unknown quantity and as their government refuses to assist the investigation, they are definitely a possibility. The fact the youngest one's mother was waiting in Frankfurt airport is immaterial in my book, as there are plenty instances of Jihadists lying to family members in order to conceal what they are about to do.

One of the London bombers was newly married and had just had a child, and he had told his wife he would see her that night, and even went as far as discussing options for the evening meal with her. Most jihadists are extremely secretive of their plans and reveal nothing of their intentions to anyone not involved in the Jihad, even to those they love, as they realise it could, and probably would, jeopardise their mission. It could perhaps leave their loved ones open to a charge of aiding and abetting someone in the plotting of a terrorist attack, so for this reason, you might not want to read too much into the Iranian passengers mother being left standing at the airport in Frankfurt. The fact is there probably would have been some sort of indication by now if this was a terrorist attack that was planned by an established Islamic group intent on a Jihad, either from one of the Government authorities or the terrorist organisation themselves, who routinely admit their attacks, almost as a recruiting tool.

There is one exception to this however. If the Iranian Government/Military wanted to attack the American Base at Diego Garcia, with perhaps the intention of destroying the drone capability there, this would be the perfect way to attack it and have total deniability. The attack would be, most likely, written off as another terrorist outrage, and the Iranian Government would never be thought of as the planners and implementers of this act of war. I think this might be the best explanation yet, as it would be imperative that the US Government hid this from the world. If they did not, they would be forced by US citizens to retaliate to this attack once Americans found out they had been attacked by a foreign country. The US. is not in a financial, or military capable position, to attack Iran at this point in time, their economy has been in real distress for a number of years, with unemployment at record levels not seen since the great depression of the 1920s, and borrowing is at an all time high.

The good news is that the economy is showing signs of recovery and when you add that to the fact that oil prices are finally dropping to a level that will help their balance of trade deficit, then anyone can see, a war with Iran is actually the last thing the Middle East or the USA needs just now. I think the President realised this immediately, and put in place the order to cover up this attack on Americans by the Iranians so that he would not have to go to war with them at this time. There is a very good chance that, firstly, an attack by America and her allies on Iran would spread to the already greatly politically unstable areas in the Middle East and Africa and fairly soon could end in a global war. Secondly, any attack on Iran would drive oil prices higher than they have ever been, and the U.S. economy, which is still fragile due to their enormous debt problems, would never be able to survive that. More importantly the Russian economy depends on high oil prices, and the increasing tension caused by Russia's military actions in the Ukraine and the Crimean Peninsula between America and Russia had led to financial sanctions being imposed on Russia's ruling elite, and low oil prices are the perfect way to ramp up this sanction pressure. Thirdly, The American President has been attempting to bring Iran in on Americas' side in the war against the increasingly powerful and dangerous Islamic State fighters, and had written a personal letter to the Ayatollah seeking help in this matter. Believe it or not, the covert operation to hide the attack on Diego Garcia from the world, and to deceive the families of the deceased on board ... could be simple economics.

5. copilot and pilot acting as a team to take the flight.

One would think at the outset that this would take an almost impossible sequence of events for not one but two pilots that were intent on joining the Jihad to find themselves in the same cockpit at the same time, it is however very possible.

Throughout the world and on every continent there are paedophiles. An utter scourge of mankind and they are rightly hunted by police forces in virtually every country. These people fully realise that if they are exposed for the horrendous acts against children that they are involved in, their lives will be ruined. Many of them have happy family lives and have excellent jobs. They fill every corner of society, and many of them have much to lose by pursuing their paedophile tendencies, yet they continue to do this and, despite the huge personal risks involved, have time again been shown to be able to organise themselves into networks of paedophiles, sometimes with sub-networks. These people have been able to do this over the Internet, and continue to do so today. They have even been known to organise the abuse of children on different continents, sometimes for years, without detection, and show an almost unbelievable level of trust in relative strangers, or even people they have never met before, and have been able to connect with each other worldwide, as long as that person has been vouched for by another paedophile. The point I am trying to make is that if paedophiles can find one another around the world and communicate successfully, then so can terrorists.

It may well be the case that the pilot and copilot, have in fact, quietly been supporters of the global jihad, independent of each other, and may have by some quirk of language and perhaps discussion over a period of months begun to understand they shared a common belief ...and then they might have devised this jihad in face-to-face meetings just the two of them, leaving no electronic trace. They would undoubtedly have time together away from the cockpit voice recorder in their hotel rooms on overnight stops to work out the details of their plan. Once they had decided to join the Jihad, all that was required of them was to wait, and they may well have waited until they were roistered together that night on Flight MH 370. The plan is extremely easily carried out. No one could stop them.

They would take off and climb to the 35,000ft cruising altitude, and proceed to the communication handover point, where they would execute their plan to hijack the flight – or steal the flight is perhaps more accurate – by first of all switching off the ACARS transponder beacon, and then a simple final communication to Malaysian Air Traffic Control as they approached the edge of the Malaysian air space. All that was left at this stage was a very simple task, which was to then switch off the communications. At this point the pilots' plans become extremely callous. Firstly switch on the passenger seat belt sign and thus ensure everyone is seated. Then instruct the cabin crew to be seated and seat-belted also. A short excuse given for this is up-coming turbulence, then simply switch the cabin pressurisation control to manual, turn hard left and put the plane up to 45,000 feet, the instant the cabin air pressure started to drop the emergency replacement air masks would be deployed automatically, further reason for everyone to be seated as you cannot leave your seat area with these still attached to your face.

The passengers and cabin crew would be extremely anxious in this situation, but it would not be for long, as the drop down emergency masks are fully depleted of all air in about ten minutes, and after that there would be no hope of survival. That would leave the two pilots in control, and shortly after the passengers died of asphyxiation, then so would the cabin crew, as their pressurised cylinders would also deplete, after approximately fifteen minutes. So the aeroplane could have been taken in this way. After some twenty minutes at 45,000 feet they would sharply decrease the altitude of the aeroplane down to 12,000 feet so they would be able to remove their replacement air masks and stabilise the cabin air pressure. Then switch the cabin pressurisation switch back to auto in case they had to climb higher than 12,000 feet again for some reason. A turn north out the centre of the Andaman Sea to avoid the civilian radar, and then continue to descend to 5,000 feet in order to avoid radar detection.

The fact that they were picked up by the strong radar signals from the Thai and Malaysian military radar seems to be immaterial, as both radar operators and military hierarchy chose to do nothing, probably because of an inbuilt belief that no one would attack them as no one has for so long. I have no doubt that there has been a tremendous shake up in both Malaysian and Thai militaries regarding their handling of this situation, the apathy that both sets of militaries conveyed that night must have worried the Politicians in Kuala Lumpur and Bangkok.

The pilots would then have continued northeast, until they were well passed the possible reach of the Indonesian commercial radar, at which point they would have turned southwest and set a heading for the Maldives, as this would help mask their final intended target, and only once they had reached the Maldives would they then turn southeast and head for Diego Garcia, probably at an altitude significantly lower than the 5,000 feet they had been flying at, thus giving them the best possible chance of going un-noticed towards their intended crash target.

It is worthy of note that neither of the crew had shown an increased interest in Islam and had not increased their number of visits to their Mosques in the weeks preceding flight MH 370 going missing. We cannot read too much into this. There is no set behavioural pattern that jihadists follow as there are again ample cases of suicide bombers and people planning on joining the Jihad actually showing an apparent decrease in their interest in Islam and the Mosque in the months and weeks prior to their actual attacks. The terrorists that took the planes in the September the Eleventh attacks hardly used the mosques once they were in the United States, they spent most of their spare time drinking alcohol, going to night clubs and frequenting prostitutes ... hardly the behaviour of a committed Islamist committed to the Jihad one would think, however it has been proven to be fairly normal behaviour. If anything about that can be said to be normal.

The copilot himself, Fariq Abdul Hamid, was described by his family as a religious man and had shown no sign of radicalisation, or in fact any sign of any change of personality, or normal behaviour, in the weeks before the 4 March flight. Once again, this has in fact been done many times before. Some jihadists, have talked about finding an inner calm, and great sense of peace with the world, once they have committed themselves to jihad, which actually makes them more easy to be around in the weeks coming up to their attack. However it might just as easily be a sign that he was in fact in no way involved.

I have already stated that I believe if either of the pilots or both were involved then the only reasons I can think of for the US President ordering the CIA to cover up the attack, as opposed to just admit it is that they did not want the potential financial backlash around the world from being responsible for the shooting down of an aeroplane full of innocent people. They also wanted to avoid any retaliatory actions against American civilians and that the US Military might want to hide their top secret satellite capability for tracking aeroplanes with their transponders off.

That is no small thing if you think about it, the ability to covertly track all your enemies military flights could give the US a huge amount of intelligence as regards troop positions and re-deployments, numbers of troops and what military hardware they have. There is no doubt that the US Military and Government could probably have admitted this attack and omitted to mention the secret satellite capability, so for me, I actually believe that neither of the pilots were involved, and I believe the Iranian Government was to blame. Furthermore I firmly believe that two pilots committed to Jihad would definitely equal two aeroplanes being hijacked, absolutely no doubt about that.

6. *Passenger and either copilot or pilot worked as a two-man team to take the plane.*

A 'clean' jihadist, or perhaps two with false passports, would certainly prove easier to place on the flight with a flight crew member committed to jihad, than it would be to organise to put two committed to that cause in the cockpit at the same time. There are various pros and cons to his argument. Firstly one of the most curious things about this flight is the obvious timing of the hijack. This was done at a very, very specific moment, with only a hand full of minutes, two in fact, between the moment that the final communication was sent to Malaysian Air Traffic Control and the introduction of themselves and the plane to the Vietnamese Air Traffic Control. This timing would be very difficult, if not impossible to guarantee, if one of the pilots was acting alone.

Put very simply, whichever pilot you believe was involved would have to ensure that his counterpart was outside the cockpit security door, just at the time of the hijack. Any notion that he could have been locked out a long time before that is wrong. The communications to

Flight MH 370 were intact until after the final hand off by whoever was flying to Malaysian Air Traffic Control and if one of the pilots found himself locked out the cockpit by his colleague then he would have used the satellite air-phone to phone his employer, Malaysian Airlines. This phone is switched on permanently as long as communications are still switched on. The fact that no call came through tells us without doubt that the plane was hijacked at a very specific point in its flight.

Whoever took the plane had to ensure that the other pilot present was locked out of the cockpit and still did not suspect there was anything untoward happening. There is no doubt that the timing required to make sure of this would prove extremely difficult if the pilot involved was acting alone. How could one pilot suggest to another he leave the cockpit and be confident he would say yes at that exact time within that very small window of opportunity? One could suggest to the other that he go for a toilet break perhaps? But what if he were to say 'No' that would leave you with no chance to make the hijack within the perfect time window that this flight obviously followed. In the case of this hijack there is no doubt a second and even third Jihadists would be advantageous in getting the other pilot out of the cabin at the perfect time. The fact that the plane was taken at the perfect time in the radar black area and at the communication hand over point, is far too much of a coincidence for most peoples' liking, and other Jihadists on board would have no doubt helped with this timing issue.

So how could one or two Jihadist helpers, hidden amongst the passengers on board, ensure the non Jihadist pilot was left in the cockpit alone during this very tight window of time?

In flight protocol dictates that if there is an onboard disturbance, such as a fight between two passengers or if there is a seriously heated argument that looks like it could get out of control, the cabin crew are instructed to intervene, and are in fact highly trained in how to do so. They are taught how to physically restrain the protagonists if necessary. They are further taught to call upon the help of the pilot or copilot to assist them if they feel they are physically overwhelmed, and as a final resort, they are taught to enlist the help of passengers to help physically subdue the people involved, basically by weight of numbers.

The passengers are to be enlisted as a last resort, after the spare pilot, as any injuries suffered during this fight/confrontation would no doubt lead to enormous lawsuits, which the airlines would want to avoid. In the event of a significant disturbance the copilot would usually be released by the pilot to help the cabin crew to subdue the perpetrators, and even in the more extreme cases, to overpower them and manacle them to their seats. There are in fact steel handcuffs on all international flights now specifically for this purpose. Now if this argument or fight was staged by two fit young men ... of Middle Eastern appearance, throwing in the odd 'jihad' word here and there, the crew could be easily frightened into believing there was an attempted hijacking in progress. This information would be immediately relayed to the cockpit, and would almost certainly result in the captain releasing the copilot to assist the cabin crew in subduing the men fighting. The cabin crew that night was made up mostly of women, and as the copilot was a fit young man, he would almost certainly have been released to help the female cabin crew deal with the situation. This way the two muscle jihadists, acting with the jihadist pilot could very accurately dictate when the cockpit was vacated by the copilot, and this could have been done to coincide with the plane approaching the communication hand over point, and that way ensured the timing of the mission was adhered to.

Similarly if the copilot was the Jihadist involved, he could have very easily tricked the pilot into believing he had a fairly serious injury that night, such as a back problem, or torn muscles in his shoulder, and he that he may have stressed to the pilot as the flight was progressing that it was becoming unbearable and was in fact debilitating. Thus when the need arose for someone to physically engage the two men fighting it was in fact the pilot himself that decided to go sort it out, as he was trained to make these on the spot calculations as to the best course of action in a crisis. The point I am trying to make is that it could have been done; it could have been manipulated so that either of the pilots were removed from the cockpit.

Either way, if one of them was tricked into leaving the cockpit. The person left flying the plane would then have immediately switched the ACARS transponder beacon off. Simultaneously he would send his final communication to the Malaysian Air Traffic Control. The person then flying the plane would immediately switch the communication switch to the off position in order to stop any communication from any member of the cabin crew, and stop them phoning in a distress call to the Malaysian Airline, via the cabin crew air phone. This way the flight was taken at the exact time it needed to be. As I outlined above the two pilots acting together could have done this, but Jihadists working without the help of one of the flight crew would have no way of timing the cockpit storming so perfectly ... they could not know to the level of accuracy needed that they were attacking at the correct time, that would have been pure luck.

As I have said before, once the person flying the aeroplane was locked into the cockpit, there is very little that could be done to stop him. The cabin pressurisation switch turned from auto to manual and a drastic climb to 45,000 feet would kill everyone except the person flying the plane, as he would then have free access to both pilots pressurised cylinder replacement air and could therefore outlast everyone else on board comfortably. The cabin crew supplies of pressurised air in their portable face masks is quite small and can only last ten or fifteen minutes, if the plane was less full of passengers. The fact the aeroplane stayed up at 45,000 feet during the initial deviation from course for a reported twenty-three minutes is probably due to the person flying the plane making sure that everyone was in fact dead, even if they could have access to two portable face masks.

In fact once the plane has come under the control of anyone with the intention of murder/suicide then I am afraid all hope is lost as regards passengers surviving. This was proved on September the Eleventh when the passengers on United Airlines flight 93 fought back heroically against the terrorists in the cockpit only to die trying to regain control of the aeroplane. In that instance they had to fight their way through Islamic terrorists armed with razor sharp Stanley knives but only a relatively flimsy cockpit door, in this instance they would have to breach a virtually impenetrable door whilst being asphyxiated. There simply would not be sufficient time for the passengers or cabin crew to do anything to alter the pilot's course of action.

7. *Either pilot or co pilot gained control of the aeroplane.*

Either pilot or co pilot gained control of the aeroplane and then flew to 45,000 ft, whereby the passengers and other crew members were asphyxiated, then lowered the planes height to 12,000 ft at which point he re-programmed the auto pilot to fly into the southern ocean and himself simply opened the rear emergency exit and jumped out ... parachuting into the jungle area in the north of Malaysia. This was a jihad mission that allowed the pilot involved to survive, and then make his way to the Middle East to re-join the Jihad.

Now at the outset this looks improbable, however, it is actually one of the simplest plans to implement, and there is a historic precedent for a mid air hijack and the assailant, a one DB Cooper parachuting from a passenger airliner over a densely wooded area.

Cooper has become an almost cult figure in America ...there is in fact a DB Cooper day where thousands still turn out to celebrate his daring heist, although it is widely felt amongst law enforcement in America, that he perished that night, after jumping from the plane. This view is held because the ransom money he was paid in, had each and every serial number noted, as a way of perhaps retrospectively catching the assailant. These notes have never been used since that night and have remained out of circulation since then, although some children found a large bundle of them washed up onto a lakeshore in the area he was felt to have jumped into ... law enforcement believing he perished in the lake. There is no doubt that this is a fanciful explanation for the plane going missing, but it does at least give the perpetrator of the hijack the chance of escape, which none of the other scenarios really does, save perhaps the hidden plane theory.

This scenario would require that the aeroplane was hijacked and that the passengers and crew were murdered as before, and that the pilot still had time to jump whilst the aircraft was over land above the Malaysian Peninsula. The jump, and parachute into jungle terrain is extremely hazardous, and the hijacker would have needed specialised training to pull it off. Broken bones are common and an injury in that region, of that severity, whilst alone, would undoubtedly have resulted in an agonisingly slow death.

Similarly a hung up parachute would require a 'rapelling device' in order to lower oneself to the jungle floor. The method used when lowering oneself from a hung up parachute is relatively straight forward, it basically requires that the rappelling rope end is attached to the parachute parachords, this can be done by knotting the end of the rappelling rope and then individually cutting each of the parachords one at a time, and tying it firmly below the knotted end of the rappelling rope, which is threaded through the donut, which is clipped to the parachute harness already on the parachutist.

The result of this is that the parachutist is then attached to the hung up parachute by the harness he is wearing and the donut, which is attached to the rappelling rope. The free end is held down in the arrest, or stop, position. Once the final parachord has been cut you are left suspended by the rappelling rope which is tied to the parachords, leaving you suspended in mid-air free of the parachute canopy, and then able to lower yourself to the ground safely and easily ... these rappelling harnesses are widely available and were designed to be used in the oil rig industry after the Piper Alpha disaster showed a need for people lowering themselves quickly and safely to the water in the event of a serious fire ... they were designed to hold even very large individuals and are fairly idiot proof ... a typical one hour course is required to familiarise oneself with the idiosyncrasies of the donut. Flight and cabin crew are meant to be subject to the same airport security as passengers are, but I am convinced that there is no way that this is administered in the same thorough atmosphere. I believe a flight crew member would probably get away with a parachute and rappelling donut in his flight bag or carry-on luggage and a simple explanation, if anyone even bothered to ask, would suffice. Flight crew, and in fact, cabin crew carry all of their luggage onto the flight with them, with none going in the hold, generally for easiness and speed of getting on and off the plane. When was the last time you saw a flight attendant standing at the carousel waiting on their luggage? So they often carry unusual items in their luggage allowance for family members or as gifts for friends, these items would not be flagged as significant, and this is therefore very plausible.

Furthermore there is ample food and water on board the flight to sustain the hijacker on the ground. The method for parachuting with this is also very simple and straightforward. There are ample passengers bags in the overhead lockers but really any bag would do ... this is filled with mostly water and some food to sustain him on his journey out of the jungle to his rendezvous point with his fellow jihadists. Once the parachute is harnessed onto the hijacker he attaches a ten foot or 3 metre piece of thin rope to his ankle and the other end to the handle of the bag. He carries the bag for the initial jump, usually across his chest, and once free of the plane releases it to fall below him ... remember falling items fall at the same speed unless wind resistance causes one to slow more rapidly towards terminal velocity , so there would be no jerk on one ankle from the bag , it would merely fall alongside until the parachute deployment chord was pulled , at this point it falls below the parachutist and dangles down underneath him hitting the ground moments before he does.

None of this is particularly taxing or requisite of great levels of skill or physical dexterity – in fact DB Cooper himself was in his forties to fifties by witness approximation. However it would require a huge supply of 'bottle', or courage, to parachute jump from an aeroplane cruising at 400 miles per hour at night. This is a fearsome task and one that would trouble any recreational parachutist. It would require great levels of selfbelief and dedication to the task. Remember the parachutist is in fact already travelling at four hundred miles per hour in the plane so the air speed across the wings would be less downwind but greater into a head wind, either way jumping into an approximate four hundred mile per hour vortex at 12,000 feet where the air is quite dense, is just about as severe a parachute exit as anyone could handle. This has actually been done often in trials by special forces around the world, in fact firstly by the Special Air Service where two volunteers dropped out of the bomb bay doors of a buccaneer fighter/bomber at 400 miles an hour – them both stating amidst a flurry of bad language that they would never do that again. It has been trialled again and again but the more recent results are classified.

The combination of dense air and air speed vortex, specifically, spinning air off the back of an aeroplane, would make this a very risky proposition for anyone but a highly trained, probably ex military operative, which neither pilot was. No one has mentioned that any member of the passengers or crew had any kind of specialised military training and I feel sure this would have been reported by now, but it cannot be stated as fact that none did.

Regardless of how absurd this potential scenario may sound we must look at it as a possibility. So if we concede that the hijacker in this case would have to be one of the pilots, to allow the hijacker the ability to carry on board his parachute and rappelling donut, then agreed that either of the pilots could take the flight and then easily murder everyone else on board. We are left with a need to find an acceptable motive for this crime. DB Cooper staged his mid-air hijack for money. It was a robbery and nothing more or less, he demanded a ransom and it was paid. His motivation was money. It would appear that money is not the deciding motivation here though, as there is simply not enough on board … if he decided to rob the corpses of the dead passengers and crew … what would that net him? … at a guess of £150 per head … £30,000 to £40,000 – say 50,000 to 60,000 US Dollars … hardly worth all the risk and certainly not enough to disappear for the rest of your life with, and let us not forget that the pilots were both earning a good wage in their respective positions and would be earning at least that per year in their current jobs.

I think we can rest assured that if there were any diamond dealers on board carrying a couple of million pounds worth of jewels with them, we would have heard about it by now. Most would concur that this does not make any sense I'm afraid and he would not have had time to rifle the dead bodies corpses and exit the plane whilst still over Malaysian land, so the robbery theory is out for sure ... not enough time ... not enough money. The only motivation I believe then would be a Jihad. This would explain the callous disregard for innocent life, and the lack of need for financial gain, as the perpetrator would no doubt be determined to re-join his Jihad comrades in another part of the world and continue fighting – Jihadists simply are not motivated by money.

This theory along with the hijack and landing at a hidden landing strip do however provide a way the hijacker could steal the plane and survive himself – all the other theories end in him dead.

8. *Aeroplane strayed out of its correct flight path.*

Aeroplane strayed out of its correct flight path due to pilot error and the US Military or Thai Military shot the plane down over the South China Sea by accident. Both Governments then conspired to cover up the accident.

Military blunders of this magnitude do happen, they have happened in the past and they will happen again. History has shown us that Governments, and even democratic Governments, are never very truthful when it comes to the aftermath of something as catastrophic as this. The Russian Military flatly denied shooting down a

Korean passenger jet full of innocent civilians for quite a while after the event, until they were embarrassed by the American satellite and radar data into admitting they had done it. The Americans have themselves made this mistake on more than one occasion and I was definitely left with the impression then when I heard them speak, that if the opportunity to deny their involvement had offered itself they would have grasped it with both hands. As it was, they also capitulated, and confessed to their involvement and their guilt, and subsequently offered an apology to the bereaved families. That is not to say that that could have happened here.

Flight MH 370 did have its transponder and communications disabled, and we cannot definitively say why. It could have been a malfunction it may have been deliberately switched off by someone in the cockpit. The Americans and the Thai were conducting missile tests and air-to-air warfare simulations and live fire test shoots at drones in the Gulf of Thailand that night. If Flight MH 370 was to have strayed into that area by mistake with all its communications and ACARS Transponder disabled then some people believe the aeroplane may have been mistaken for a drone and engaged with a long distance air-to-air missile and shot down. I personally cannot accept this scenario. These air combat simulations with live ammunition are organised under the strictest of military safety. Overhead there is always an AWAC Airborne Warning and Control radar capable aeroplane. The AWAC is put in place so that the pilots flying the fighter aeroplanes can have their performances critiqued by their superiors; it basically gives an overview of the simulated battlefield, just as they would have in real life. The AWAC has an enormous array of the worlds' most powerful, sophisticated and sensitive targeting and acquisition systems ever invented, and anyone that suggests a slow moving passenger liner could sneak up on this military exercise is a lunatic. The AWACs were designed to stop people sneaking up on the US Military ... that is basically its job. There has been no wreckage sighted in this area, and it was checked by the Vietnamese coastguard very early on, as a lone man, called Mike McKay from New Zealand working on an oil rig in the South China Sea/Gulf of Thailand area did say he had witnessed a flaming aeroplane, at two o clock in the morning on that dark night, and at a distance of fifty to sixty kilometres by his estimation. There would be many explanations for what he saw that night, but my bet is it was probably a single phosphorous heat seeker countermeasure, shot from one of the military aeroplanes. At fifty kilometres there is no way he could see an aeroplane being shot down – absolutely no chance. It is simply too far away. Mr McKay described seeing the flaming aeroplane standing static in his vision, he attributed this to the aeroplane either flying towards him or away from him, and he even gave his best guess at grid reference points and flight path routes.

believe that the man saw a phosphorous grenade being deployed, these grenades sometimes explode or burst into life and they give of an enormous light and heat signature, there is a variety that is suspended by a small parachute, and they often give the impression of holding a steady altitude, or not falling downwards in layman's terms, this is easily explained; the heat given off by the phosphorous is extreme by any standard, and on a still night the air immediately around the phosphorous is superheated and rises straight up into the parachute umbrella and causes considerable lift, this dramatically reduces the fall rate of the phosphorous grenade and in certain conditions can in fact cause it to be virtually suspended in air for quite a considerable amount of time.

The light signature given off by the phosphorous grenade is very intense and could be seen at the distances the Kiwi rig worker gave, and many reports around the world from civilians claiming to have seen a UFO are subsequently explained as having been phosphorous grenades deployed from aircraft. Having worked on an oil rig myself I know they are well radar equipped, as helicopters are constantly being landed on them to ferry personnel to and from shore. It would be a simple task to access the stored data in the oil rig flight control room and verify what happened that night but I am confident that it would not show flight MH 370 being shot down and crashing into the South China Sea.

So we have explored the different ways in which the plane could have been taken. I believe the timing of the hijack to be critical, in fact I believe that timing is the key to unlocking this puzzle, it would for me, prove difficult for either the pilot or the copilot to get the other out of the cockpit at the perfect time of, just prior to the communication hand over between Malaysian air traffic control and the Vietnamese air traffic control, especially as this was less than an hour after take-off and would therefore be less likely to require one of the crew needing a comfort break or food. There is no doubt it could be achieved much easier if there were people on board hidden within the passengers that had been enlisted to cause a disturbance with the objective of getting one of the cockpit crew out ... and that could lead to the conclusion that the pilot, captain Shah was more likely involved, as he would be the one to decide who left the cockpit to assist the cabin crew in dealing with a disturbance, and as the copilot was the significantly younger man, it would be unlikely the older pilot would volunteer to go and join in a fight, as would be required if the copilot was involved in the hijack, this would leave too much to chance for me.

There is the possibility that the two pilots were involved. This would take an enormous series of coincidences to occur but it is certainly not impossible. Islamic extremists have proven for many years now to be very organised, patient and full of guile, and have infiltrated many government buildings, military bases, and secure areas around the globe– consistently. In many ways the almost extreme timing of the hijack, which was critical, would prove easiest if both pilots were involved ... however if I was an organiser of jihadist atrocities and someone high-up the decision making ladder, I would think two pilots equals two planes, and why waste two pilot jihadists on one operation? For me I would use one and organise the other into a similar position to get maximum terror effect and this reason alone proves to me that if the pilots were involved, then there was probably only one jihadist pilot on board that night. There is no way that the Jihadists that organise and run these operations would sacrifice two pilots for one mission.

It is possible that one member of the crew drugged the other, perhaps by dropping sleeping tablets, which are permissible in carry-on luggage, into the cockpit coffee thermos flask. This is also feasible. The plane had taken off and safely climbed to cruising altitude, a reasonably stressful part of the journey, the auto pilot is engaged and all systems are normal, either the captain offers the copilot or vice versa a cup of coffee, remember, both men are Muslim and don't drink alcohol, and coffee or tea is commonly taken and shared amongst Muslim men as they chat. It was a late flight and the stimulant effect the coffee would have would be welcome, and it would mask the taste of sleeping pills. This is also a real possibility and one that could no doubt have successfully allowed one or the other to take the cockpit almost silently, and without the cabin crew having any idea of what was happening. Drugged to sleep or poisoned to death, the end result would be the same anyway. This method of taking control of the cockpit would be the easiest and the critical timing, which was so important, could be adhered to.

Similarly, if one of the pilots was to have killed the other, perhaps during the first half hour of the flight where all communications between the cabin crew and cockpit are banned, then this could also leave either one in the perfect situation to take the aeroplane at the critical time.

Many people will be thinking that Jihadists would have chosen a target nearer to hand, perhaps somewhere in Thailand, in which to crash the plane. Phuket Island, and especially Patong Beach there, are constantly full of foreign tourists from around the globe, and could have easily been attacked that night, but I believe the Jihadists on board that night wanted to strike at America and kill Americans. There is only one target in the entire Far East where the pilots could guarantee, without question of being full of Americans at that time of night, remember it was shortly after one in the morning and all the US

Embassies throughout the Far East would be virtually deserted and that would be the Indian Ocean Island American Military base on Diego Garcia.

Diego Garcia is in fact a British overseas territory having been purchased by the British in 1953 from the Maldives, and was subsequently leased to the United States Government and by extension the US Military, so they can use it as a forward operating base for aircraft and un-manned drones in the Arabian gulf, it is home to 3,000 US military personnel responsible for keeping all kinds of aircraft serviced and repaired, people like cooks, aircrew, loadies, pilots, etc ... it is in fact a hugely impressive base.

The CIA are alleged to have used the base as a hidden backwater for torturing suspected jihadists during the ten years immediately after the September 11 attack on New York. It is, sadly, a beautiful Island with a terrible past, and would no doubt have ended up being a competitor for the Maldives and the Seychelles as a holiday destination had it not been leased to the Americans. It has a very long runway and large areas of the island are covered with buildings, which vary in uses from dormitories to aircraft hangers, it looks from certain angles as if it is almost bursting at the sides.

A hijacked Boeing 777 crashing into one of the buildings anywhere on this island, save perhaps one of the aircraft hangers, would have caused mass casualties, simply because it is so densely populated. This would explain why the plane having reached 45,000 feet in order to murder the passengers and crew then dropped down to 12,000 feet as the pilot needed to reach an altitude where he could breathe and settle himself, and then on down to 5,000 feet so he could defeat any radar on his way to his objective. If he had simply wished to commit suicide then why turn around? Surely he would have simply plunged the plane into the sea as have the other two pilots that have committed these murder/suicide by aeroplane atrocities.

If this was a hijacking for political reasons as has been hinted at by the media, then what political purpose did it satisfy? In fact if there was a political motivation to this at all it hasn't been explained in any way, and the whole point of a political motivated act is to make a statement and there has been no statement of a political nature that we have had our attention drawn to. So what is the motivation to do it politically? Surely a political statement needs to have a direct point and I think he would have left a letter somewhere at least with an explanation to put forward his political point of view. Otherwise his big political statement has no statement.

So it looks like a jihadist or jihadists took the plane as their statement is in fact the act itself, so no explanatory notes are left or needed.

It is my belief the hijacker/s underestimated the capabilities of the US Military to track aeroplanes with their transponders off across an area of open ocean. He/they may even have underestimated the resolve of the Americans, in that he may have believed the US President Barack Obama would never sanction the shooting down of a passenger liner full of people. Or that he/they may have even been able to talk his way into being allowed to land whereby he could then continue with his plan – whatever he/they surmised – he/they were wrong.

It is also my belief that the US Military tracked Malaysian flight MH 370 from shortly after take-off, as they do with every flight around the world, and once they failed to contact Vietnamese Air traffic control, and then deviated from their pre flight agreed flight path, which all flights must now produce in writing an hour prior to take off, then a computer in Cheyenne Mountain red flagged the flight as being off its designated flight path without communicating the reason why. ALL flights around the world are monitored this way and if they are watching asteroids out in space that they can do little or nothing about and that pose little or no threat to us (when was the last person you know killed by an asteroid?) then they are watching aeroplanes, for the simple reason that they have proven to be the weapon most dangerous to Americans in recent years. In fact if they aren't watching for planes that are off their flight path without communicating the reason why, then they are in dereliction of duty by my book. No, there is zero chance of this aeroplane not being tracked by the Paterson bunker complex. We also know the Americans had satellites over the area by the fact that they stated that the plane had NOT blown up in flight, and this proves, if they knew it wasn't blown up mid flight, then they MUST know where it was throughout its flight, or they couldn't have made that statement.

The flight was tracked, and the military base at Diego Garcia was contacted by the Paterson bunker complex and told to scramble fighters to intercept the jet. It would be unlikely at this stage that the order to shoot it down would have been given, as there was plenty of time left, as the plane was heading southwest on its deviated route to the Maldives and into a vast area of ocean and was many hours from anywhere. The President would have been informed. Make no mistake; this was a Presidential decision. As far as this is concerned, however, there was no decision to make. The Presidents hand would be forced and he would have to make the choice to shoot at some time.

Standard International protocol for a military fighter jet intercepting a commercial passenger jet liner is as follows.

The fighter pilot must announce his presence to whoever is flying the passenger liner by trying to speak to them on the short-wave radio. He is to use both military and civilian frequencies.

If this fails, he is to fly alongside the passenger liners cockpit at close quarters, and attempt to gain visual contact with whoever is flying the aeroplane, and failing that with anyone on board.

If the Pilot of the passenger liner fails to acknowledge the presence of the fighter, the fighter pilot will move further aside and shoot tracer rounds from the fighter's canon across and in front of the cockpit windows of the passenger liner. At night, as it was in this case, these are like large fireworks being shot in front of your car window and could never go un-noticed.

This is a clear signalling of intent to shoot down the passenger aeroplane unless they establish contact, either over the short-wave radio or visually, and once that has been done to then comply with the fighter pilot's orders. At this point one of a couple of things could have happened.

1. The hijacker or hijackers would have completely ignored the pilot's orders and failed to communicate, in which case the fighter pilot, having followed all the correct International protocols, waited for a

direct order from his superior officer as to his next course of action, and he in turn from the Secretary of Defence, and he in turn from President Obama himself. Once the decision to fire on the aeroplane had been given, and I think this would have been withheld until the aeroplane had crossed the maritime exclusion zone demarcation line, the fighter pilot would have fallen into a position a few hundred meters behind the aeroplane and executed his Presidents orders, and shot the aeroplane out the sky, probably using the canon and not the missile, as a missing missile would be harder to explain than a few canon rounds. The pilot would follow the airliner down to the sea and then radio in confirming the target had been destroyed. He would also radio in the accurate grid reference or GPS of the position of the impact into the water.

2. The hijacker or hijackers would have acknowledged the fighter pilot and have established communications over the short-wave radio, the fighter pilot would have a conversation with whoever was flying the aeroplane to try and establish what was going on. The fighter pilot would also be asking very direct questions in order to ascertain who was flying the aeroplane. The hijacker/s reasons for the deviation from the agreed flight plan, would have been relayed back to command, and as there is no other runway within the aeroplanes fuel reserve capabilities, the military hierarchy and the President would be left with a serious problem. Firstly, if we assume that the person flying the aeroplane is one of the original flight crew that have decided to join the Jihad, what acceptable reason could they give to the fighter pilot

and his command that would trick them or coerce them into allowing the aeroplane to land at the runway at Diego Garcia. It is difficult to think of any, especially as the entire compliment of the passengers would be unresponsive and not even looking out of their windows, and with this lack of reasonable excuse for being so far of course, then the military would be left with no choice but to label it a potential deadly threat to the personnel at Diego Garcia, and to shoot it down.

Secondly then, if we assume the person flying the aeroplane was not a member of the original flight crew but in fact a terrorist intent on a Jihad attack on Diego Garcia then it becomes a bit more complicated. You see a commercial airline pilot would never really have an acceptable excuse for being that far off of course even if there had been a dramatic event and loss of instruments with which to navigate the aeroplane. However an untrained passenger that had been left flying the aeroplane, after some near catastrophic event, despite having no formal training at all, could very easily have become disoriented at night, as I have outlined before. If the fighter pilot questioned whoever was flying and established his identity, which they would be able to do from the passenger list, and whoever was flying the aeroplane claimed to be flying as a result of having survived this serious event then they would actually have a very good reason for being where they were, and that would make it almost impossible for the Americans to shoot the aeroplane down. Unless of course the person flying was in fact an Iranian man, flying on a false passport. There would be no way, regardless of which of his names he gave or what he said, that he would be allowed anywhere near the Island base.

Either way the end result is the same. All on board are dead, but the potential political fall-out would be incredible. The political backdrop to Flight MH 370 going missing was quite tense with the Russians, under President Putin, in the process of annexing the Crimean Peninsula from the Ukraine. America and her allies are involved in a multi-national attempt to put pressure on Putin financially and to politically isolate Russia for acting in a 'unilateral and aggressive manner'. Difficult words to defend if the fact that the President had ordered a plane full of potentially alive international civilians shot out of the sky, in order to protect an American military installation, had come out.

Also the future potential for retaliatory terrorist attacks against American civilians would be huge and not just from jihadists, who are trying their best to do this anyway, but also from governments who had people from their country on board. There is in fact a precedent where this has happened before this event; Iran Air Flight 655, a passenger airliner, was shot down by the US Vincennes by accident whilst on its way to Dubai Airport from Tehran with the tragic loss of 290 lives, included amongst the dead were 66 children. This caused a huge outcry in Iran and much vengeance was called for by the Iranian people. It has been alleged by the Americans that the Iran Air Flight was transmitting on an incorrect frequency and had their transponder switched off as they were approaching the airspace of the US

Vincennes, the Americans claim that the Vincennes had tried to establish contact with the aeroplane on both commercial and military frequencies to establish their intentions, however the aeroplane remained un-responsive which led the US. missile destroyer to engage them with the Aegis missile defence system, resulting in the aeroplane being destroyed with the loss of everyone on board, and the aeroplane crashing into the Arabian Gulf.

America has consistently denied this was the fault of the Captain of the Vincennes, as other ships in his battle group, the USS Sides and USS Montgomery had that morning come under fire by Iranian gunboats whilst in international waters, subsequent to this the Vincennes had followed the Iranian gunboats into Iranian waters in pursuit to try to engage them. Confusion had ensued, in which the Iranian passenger jet was mistaken for an Iranian Military fighter and was wrongly shot down. Iranian hardliners standing beside the Ayatollah demanded reprisals and an operation was put in action. Pan Am Flight 103 was subsequently destroyed by a bomb over the Scottish town of Lockerbie and this was their retribution for the downed Iran Air flight 655.

Subsequently the Americans and British, secret services showed staggering levels of incompetence, and bungled the investigation. Most intelligent people and in fact many of the relatives of the dead passengers believe that a Libyan patsy by the name Al Magrahi was jailed wrongly, on dubious evidence. He was released shortly before his death on compassionate grounds, much to the annoyance of the Americans. He has since died. No Iranians have ever been charged or named in connection with the Lockerby atrocity, another case of America being frightened to stand up to their leadership, despite the fact that I believe they support acts of terrorism against American targets.

Furthermore, it is important to mention the fact that there were American citizens on board, three of them, and an American President cannot make the decision to end their lives without anything other than an iron clad, solid reason, as they are constitutionally protected under American Law, and the political fall-out in the States would be huge if it could be proved he acted unlawfully. That could bring down the Presidency.

Of course if the Iranians were involved in this, as an act of terrorism aimed at the US Military, and sponsored by the Iranian Regime, that would be a very compelling reason for the President of the United States, not to allow the truth to come out.

I believe that these are the reasons the Americans have tried to cover this up. What might seem like a difficult task is in fact relatively simple. Here is how it would be done. The whole episode, from the moment the flight is red flagged at Paterson Air force Base is classed as top secret. Anyone divulging any information about this incident would face the severest of prison sentences, without any hope of a fair trial. The U.S. Military are very good at the carrot and the stick where this is concerned, and recent sentences in the courts of the United States for people daring to breach the strict secrecy codes of the Military and Government bare testimony to this, with ridiculously harsh, long prison sentences being handed out, most of which is to be spent in solitary confinement, which in many cases leads to serious mental issues, this is the stick

And of course there is promotion, and cleansing of one's service record, and preferential transfers to good bases and jobs, this is the carrot.

There is little doubt that it would be hugely advantageous for anyone's career if they were to shut up and follow orders.

An important point to note is that it is my belief that the plane would have been shot down within the territorial waters of Diego Garcia. This is the only way the Americans could ensure none of the wreckage was discovered by deep sea fisherman working in the Indian Ocean, which is in fact teaming with Japanese fishing vessels many with enormous nets that stretch for many dozens of miles. Without a doubt, any errant piece of wreckage, say a seat cover or other recognisable piece of floating debris that found its way into these nets would have destroyed the next part of the Americans' illusion.

The Islands have the protection of being British overseas territories and therefore no one can fish the waters around the Islands without permission from both the British and the Americans, which would never be allowed. I am convinced that if this indeed did happen then the US President would have at some point told his Malaysian Presidential counterpart Najib Razak what had happened to Flight MH 370. He may have altered the story a little and worded it in a way that would convince the old President to play along, but I am sure they shared a reasonably close version of the truth. In fact I am fairly sure he was spoken to about this by Barrack Obama on 23 March.

The reason for this is that the very next morning on 24 March, in Kuala Lumpur we heard PM Razak declare, '...that all the worlds aviation experts had come to the same conclusion that Flight MH 370 had ended in the deep Southern Indian Ocean, and all lives were lost, without any hope of survivors.' If we examine this statement there are very illuminating points.

I think he subconsciously said Southern 'Indian' Ocean as that was where Obama had told him, and not the Southern Ocean, which is incredible as they are quite different bodies of water, and every search to that date had been in the Southern Ocean, and not the Indian Ocean, as that is where the satellite data had pointed to, this may well have been a slip of the tongue.

The most incredible part of his statement made that morning was his utter assuredness that everyone on board was dead, how could he know that? One would think it would be utterly impossible for him to say that with so much conviction, without proof, and as no wreckage had been found; what proof did he have? Indeed an emaciated man, barely alive, was washed up on the Marshal Islands in January this very year, having spent 16 months afloat in a small fishing boat, without any supplies to sustain him, he had to make improvised funnels out of plastic sheeting to catch rainwater to drink, and caught and ate fish to survive his ordeal, and had covered 12,500 kilometres during this time, having been washed offshore by strong winds and waves whilst fishing just off-shore from the West coast of Mexico. This would at least confirm that people could survive in life rafts for extended periods in the open ocean.

How could he know the plane didn't successfully land in the water and the passengers were alive in life rafts, as the aeroplane did in the Hudson River in New York the previous year?

How could he know that even if the aeroplane had crashed into the sea that no one had survived, not even one person, and had climb into the life rafts of the aeroplane?

These are automatically deployed in water, how could he Know?

How could he know that the aeroplane had not come down in an area of ocean close to some of the small uninhabited Islands in the Indian Ocean and survivors had made their way ashore?

There is only one way he could have known that all the crew and passengers were dead. He knew they were all dead because President Obama told him, and President Obama knew because the CIA had already begun to fish the remains of the passengers out of the water along with the wreckage of Flight MH 370 and knew that everyone had died, and that is an almost undeniable piece of evidence that Prime Minister Razak had been told by someone who had access to information directly from the crash site.

Was this a second slip of the tongue by an old man under the most intense pressure he has ever experienced? The incredible scrutiny they were finding themselves under over the missing flight, combined with the fact that they had only just managed to hold onto political power in Malaysia, having been run very close by his most capable political opponent ever. The same political opponent having been jailed for five years on what most people felt were trumped up charges, and this was further undermining their political position.

Did Obama persuade him that the jihad hijack was best loosely reported as a politically motivated crime by his most serious adversaries' relation, and that this would help raise the profile of the case against his opponent to a place where more Malaysians would look on his opponent unfavourably, and perhaps lessen the political impact from people about the fake charges that had been brought against the opposition?

International lies from the top of the tree?

This would explain many things. In order to cover up the shooting down of flight MH 370 at Diego Garcia an alternate crash site would need to be found. The American CIA had a hand in all of this. They have some of the most capable computer experts and hackers in the world working for them. Data could be altered to show the flight had flown longer and therefore further. Do you remember the initial reports from the Inmarsat people stated the flight had flown for four hours more after the communications were ended? Then they said five hours, then seven hours, and then even eight hours, how on earth could they have miscounted that?

Utter rubbish, there is no way that could be missed and I believe that perhaps the data was being altered by someone working for the CIA, who have tremendous hacking ability, so that they could extend the time the aeroplane flew, so that they could convince the world it had flown really far south into the Southern Ocean, and into the most inhospitable, and difficult piece of ocean on the planet, where search crews would be able to search for days and not find anything, but no one's suspicions would be raised.

Firstly the Americans and the Malaysians would need to buy time as the necessary clean up of wreckage debris from the waters around the Diego Garcia Island base would take some time and how better to buy some than a complete diversion of the whole search area into an utterly inhospitable part one of the deepest Oceans in the world, fifteen hundred miles from the nearest landmass. This clean up would be a CIA operation, they have proved many times over the years that they are capable of such tasks without any sign of information leaks, out-with the operation, which would be absolutely vital in this case as nothing could be missed, One stray piece of identifiable wreckage that could be tied to the MH 370 flight, such as a passport or passenger wallet with credit cards, would undoubtedly cause huge suspicion if it turned up in a part of the Indian Ocean, nowhere near the area that authorities were telling the world that they were sure the plane had crashed in.

I believe the Americans initially misguided the Malaysian investigators to the Southern Ocean, it is an unbelievable coincidence that the one piece of very, very deep water, combined with particularly rough seas was in fact the actual final resting place for this flight. 'The perfect storm of impossible search areas' as it was called by the Australian Prime Minister.

The Americans sent those investigating the missing flight into an area of water that they knew the searchers could spend two years searching if necessary, and no one would have doubted the difficulty of the task, it was said day after day, how impossible it was, how vast it was, how inhospitable it was, how remote it was, and so on…

The water was so deep the pings of the two black boxes couldn't be detected by conventional listening devises we were told, it would take the specialised towed pinger locator the Americans owned to find it in this depth of water. The water here is all deep with many parts reaching 8,000 plus meters deep, and even the shallower areas still bottoming out at a depth of 4,500 meters; well below the maximum depth of a conventional acoustic microphone which could only detect the audible pings down to a maximum depth of 2,000 meters and these pings from the black box recorders would start to fade and disappear around four weeks after they came into contact with the water. So the vital piece of search equipment that was needed was undoubtedly the towed array pinger locator, owned by the Americans.

This is a relatively small device, only measuring a metre by a metre at most, that is shaped like a 'V' with the pointed end attached to a steel cable. It has small stabiliser winglets on the rear tips of the 'V' to keep it level as it is towed through the water. This pinger locator is generally lowered into the depth of the ocean to a depth that will allow it to hear the audible 'pings' being given off by each of the black boxes. The theory being that the signal strength gets weaker the further you are from the black box generating the 'pings'. It is then a fairly straightforward process of following the strongest signal until it has pin-pointed the exact location.

Remember the depth of water here is extremely deep and so this array would need to go very deep in order to have a chance of hearing the 'pings' from the black boxes, as they can travel a maximum of 2,000 metres in water. Beyond this distance they become inaudible and undetectable due to the significant background noise that the oceans themselves generate. This was the vital piece of equipment able to get down to sufficient depth to be able to have any chance of hearing the 'pings' and thus find the data recorders, before the batteries exhausted.

It had taken a week to identify the possible location as being the Southern Ocean and the aeroplane searches started immediately from that point, aided by the satellite imagery we were shown. Yet almost incredibly, despite the fact that the batteries in the black boxes had a life of only four weeks, and were obviously the most serious consideration in the search at that point, specifically that, in such deep water, the pinger locator would need to be used before the batteries went flat, but instead of flying it immediately to Australia, so that it could be utilised immediately, or at least to have it ready and at hand if good information pointed the search in a specific direction, they stuck it on a ship, and whatever way you cut it there is NO excuse that fits for that. They were buying time; pure and simple.

It may even have been the case that, as this is the only towed pinger locator in the world, the CIA were in fact using it themselves to locate the black boxes at the actual crash site close to Diego Garcia. This would be absolutely vital for them to find. They would need the black boxes for the next part of their plan.

The Chinese were starting to throw huge resources at the search area in the Southern Ocean and they were being helped by the Australians and British. The Australians being the Country in charge of the search as it was the nearest landmass and everyone involved would need the ports and airports there for re-supply. The Australians never shirked their duty and, in fact, sent their search planes day after day into a very hostile area of the world and should be commended for their sense of caring for the efforts they made in their attempts to find the missing plane for the families of the bereaved.

A number of countries were helping with their spy satellites with at least five countries at the early search stage offering images from the Southern Ocean that could, perhaps hold the key, they believed, to the planes' disappearance. Daily media briefings would have us shown images from the Southern Ocean of large pieces of white coloured debris, which satellite imagery experts would have us believe were pieces of the missing planes, some of it 70 feet long or more. None of which were ever even seen by any of the search crews in the aeroplanes or boats, let alone recovered and this was despite having accurate grid references and GPS co-ordinates pin-pointing exactly where these images showed the debris to be.

We were told that oceanographers could accurately plot the currents and wind drift of debris that had been in the water for weeks by studying the historic weather over that period, and by this method point us to the scene of the crash site – well, if they could plot it back four weeks through storms and rough seas then why couldn't they plot it back one day to find the pieces the satellites allege they saw twenty-four hours earlier, utter nonsense. Then we were told it had sunk. We are asked to believe that this debris had survived for nearly three weeks in the water, afloat, having survived an enormous impact as it crashed, only to be found by a spy satellite and then miraculously sank before a plane could get to its position. It all seems very well parcelled together for me.

The fact is if that plane crashed in the water in the area we were told by the authorities then by now, without a shadow of a doubt, a verifiable piece of wreckage that could be tied to the missing flight would have been found – PERIOD – and the search crews involved, despite having enormous resources at their disposal, have not found anything from the missing plane. What a load of nonsense.

The fact is they haven't found any yet – as I write this – but I've a feeling they will soon. Not because that is where the plane crashed, but because the CIA have had four weeks now to gather the debris from the actual crash site at Diego Garcia, and

I think, will be planning to reposition it somewhere very inaccessible, probably in the deepest part of the Southern Ocean so they can deny that America had anything to do with shooting it down.

This is of course a serious allegation, even though it is a hypothetical one, but let us see if this could be done.

For this hypothetical scenario to have happened in real life there are a number of vital things that the CIA would have to do to adequately cover their tracks.

Let us remember that on board this Boeing 777 there were no less than six actual locators, not including the transponder. One each in each of the two black boxes which give off and audible ping. These are activated in contact with water and have an approximately four-week battery lifespan. There are also four emergency transmitter locators on board. These are designed to survive a plane crash and then detach themselves and float to the surface. Once on the surface they omit a signal, which is detected by satellites specifically in space for this purpose, these are owned by a company called Cospas-Sarsat, whom offers this cover worldwide. This emergency is then relayed to emergency services, and the satellite company can pinpoint the location of the floating emergency transmitter. These have a much shorter battery life of only 120 hours. The black box pingers would be an easy problem for the CIA to handle, relatively speaking. The 'ping' they give off is audio only, that is, that it is a noisemaker with no other signal that can be detected by satellites or any other detector.

So as the plane was shot down in the waters surrounding the Island of Diego Garcia then there was no need to worry about anyone else detecting the signal they gave off. The next part of the problem the black boxes pose is not so simple to deal with, but still something that the CIA could handle. The black boxes on board are quite distinct. The cockpit voice recorder only records audio, specifically everything that is said between the two pilots and anyone else that enters the cockpit during the flight. It will also pick up any ambient noise and will record any conversations with Air Traffic Controllers.

This audio recording is switched on as one of the pre flight checks, done from the pre flight checklist. It is designed to record for a minimum of two hours on a continuous loop, essentially it records for two hours, and then records over the top of what has been recorded already. This means that at any time there is always a full two hours of audio that can be listened to in the event of a crash. This would actually be a great help to the CIA. As the plane has been reported to fly on for many hours after the final communication, and most of this would be over open ocean, they would simply substitute the audio tape with one that only has no cockpit voice on it at all, and merely the noises an aeroplane makes in flight. The argument being that if the pilot or copilot took the flight they would be alone so would not be speaking to anyone as they would be alone in the cockpit. Or even more simply that the flight navigation computer was flying the plane and it would appear that no one was in the cockpit, and they do not know what happened on board.

They would need to add the fuel warning sound that would sound as the tanks ran dry, the engine warning audio as the jet engines ran out of fuel and stopped providing thrust, followed by the Master Alarm, probably an over-speed warning as the flight went nose down and sped up to a dangerously high level, and finally the Pull Up Terrain Warning you would expect to hear prior to a crash into the ocean, as the plane would sense it was falling dangerously low. No voices to fake. That is easy for them. For this reason I believe that the investigators will find the cockpit voice recorder some day. This will strengthen their argument that the flight did not crash after being shot down at Diago Garcia, and actually crashed wherever they say that it did.

The Flight Data Recorder is a different piece of equipment and now collects data from eighty-eight different sources from the aeroplane, these are basically altitude, air speed, heading, the pitch the aircraft was flying at, the amount of rudder the pilot put in, throttle used, etc. It poses a more serious problem for the CIA as it records data for twenty-five hours, which means it would have, within its data, a record of what cockpit controls were used and any various control alterations or flight control inputs done by human hand at the time around which the plane is believed to have gone off course. It would in fact have a complete record of all of the data from the entire flight.

Now I am no CIA operative but it would seem a reasonably simple task to take a similar, in fact exactly similar, Boeing 777 and fly this particular route using the known heights and speeds the original flight did, from the information collated during the course of this investigation. They could quite easily substitute anywhere in the Indian Ocean or even the Southern Ocean as the final resting place for this flight. As long as the first hour of the flight path and speed corroborated with the information they have up to the point the plane went missing. It would simply strengthen their case that the flight crashed into the ocean where they said it did. The CIA has been flying covert operations for decades, and this would be easy for them. They could even fly the suspected route and advertise the fact, and simply state that they were trying to assimilate the flight conditions to see if they could garner any more information. All too easy for an organisation that has the skill set that the CIA has. Of course they could have even thrown the breaker at the time of the hijack and the CIA could also do this and reduce the risk of any mistake. The cockpit voice recorder would be found and would have a relatively silent recording, save for the cockpit alarms sounding as the plane reached its crash site, and this would raise no red flags with the examiners.

The cockpit data recorder would corroborate all the information known about the flight to date and would show the navigation computer was responsible for flying the missing aeroplane to its crash site. This and may even point the finger at a member of the flight crew as to being the reason the flight went missing, but more likely it would leave that questioned unanswered, as this would allow for any imperfections in the CIA's operation.

So, put very simply, the two black boxes could help the CIA strengthen their story.

There have in fact been several acoustic contacts in the Southern Ocean search areas, consistent with the frequency of signal that would be sent out by the 'pings' from black boxes. Let us examine this evidence.

The scientists from the British company that own and operate the Inmarsat Satellite pointed the search teams to a very vague area in the Southern Ocean. It is an enormous area of water and unfortunately the scientists were unable to give any kind of accurate potential position, as the data they had to work with was not meant for tracking aeroplanes, it was in fact for communication. They could however give a best guess at the general whereabouts of the plane by a kind of Frankenstein use of the data they had. The search crews then called on experts in the aviation industry to try and figure out how far the aeroplane could have flown on the fuel it was known to have on board.

There are in fact huge variables in this computation, with such things as;

Altitude: this is important primarily as air density is much less the higher the altitude. This also affects air speed and ground speed. In layman's terms a flight at 35,000 feet at 450 miles per hour actual speed might use as much as a full third less fuel than a flight at the same 450 miles per hour actual speed that was flying at 5,000 feet.

Wind direction: Needless to say if an aeroplane was flying into a head wind of one hundred miles an hour at 5,000 feet, which is a very common wind speed at this altitude, it would fly an enormous distance less than if it were flying with a tail wind of one hundred miles an hour at the altitude. The difference is actually huge. Similarly, if an aeroplane was flying at 35,000 feet with a tail wind of 100 miles an hour as are very common in the jet stream at this altitude it would travel further than if it had a head wind at the same height. It is also necessary to note that an aeroplane flying through a severe cross wind is also affected as the aeroplane will tend to crab, or fly forwards at an angle to its intended flight path, and also the vertical rudder would be used to hold the aeroplane on its compass bearing and this increases drag.

Throttle ratio: This is in fact easiest explained if we draw a parallel with someone driving a car. If you were to fill your car up at the garage and then drive at twenty miles per hour till the tank was empty it would be very inefficient if you compared the miles per litre achieved, or total distance achieved, to the results you would get if you drove your car at fifty-seven miles per hour. The difference is about a third or 33% variance in actual total distance travelled. Similarly if you drove your car at full throttle it would achieve even less than if you drove the car at twenty miles per hour. Aeroplanes are no different. They have an optimum flight speed and an on board computer tells them this flight speed, which it constantly calculates throughout the flight. The difference between inefficient flight speed, generally over throttle high speed, and efficient flying speed is more than ten percent. As you can imagine aeroplanes burn fuel at alarming rates and any gadget to increase flight fuel economy is imperative to the Airlines profitability.

So, if we take the optimum flight altitude, and the optimum flight tail wind, and the optimum throttle setting for efficiency, then we have the maximum distance the aeroplane could have flown with the fuel on board, which is a known amount. We also know that the aeroplane flew north as it was supposed to after take-off, and then, after the final transmission, west across the northern part of Malaysia and the southern tip of Thailand, and then north, through the Andaman Sea, then west again, out into the Indian Ocean, then south, to its final destination. This we know from the radar data the Malaysian Government has, and it has been substantiated by other foreign military radar data, which shows the same.

The original flight to Beijing takes five hours and fifty-three minutes. Commercial passenger liners are ordered by law to carry extra fuel. The FAA regulations are very precise. A plane must take off with enough fuel to reach its primary destination airport and then its most distant alternate airport based on conditions. It must carry a further 45 minutes of fuel on top of that. Beijing International Airport was the primary destination with Beijing Capital Airport being the alternate airport only 10 minutes flying time on top of the five hour fifty minutes. A simple calculation shows the maximum flying time for fuel on board was five hours fifty-three plus ten plus forty-five, and that equals four hundred and eight minutes, or six hours and forty-eight minutes maximum flying time.

This would be the maximum flying time from Kuala Lumpur. So for the sake of argument let us say it was seven hours, the absolute maximum, as aeroplanes never carry extra fuel as it makes the plane heavier and therefore less efficient. There is no way any airline would cost itself money by carrying around tonnes of jet fuel for no reason, zero chance of that as cargo space equals profit and extra fuel equals loss. Now I am sure the more astute of you will have already noticed where I am going with this. The missing flight as we know flew north for an hour and then across Malaysia and up through the Andaman Sea which is further north and then west into the Indian Ocean, all of which, when you calculate the distance, and rely on the Thai radar signatures proves the plane was there an hour and thirty-four minutes after it took off.

So seven hours minus the ninety-four minutes for the flight time until the plane actually turned south leaves a maximum flight time of five hours and twenty-six minutes remaining. The Boeing 777 has a cruising speed of approximately five hundred and fifty miles per hour, and if we calculate the flying time left, multiplied by cruising speed of the aircraft, we get a maximum distance south of three thousand and twenty-five miles. Even if we ignore the fact it was a fully laden flight, and that the prevailing winds on the way south are mostly cross winds but some are head winds, we find we are well short of the initial search areas that the search teams were sent to, which is at least a further one thousand miles south. I was able to work that out on a laptop in ten minutes. Try it for yourself. Search Banda Ache to

Perth Australia distance. You will get the result two thousand nine hundred and nineteen miles, and the city of Perth is in Australia, and the searches were going way further south than that. Is it even remotely feasible that they could make that mistake? I mean even remotely, I do not think that is anything short of criminal. Let us not forget they were meant to be desperately looking for potential survivors at that point. I believe that someone skilfully guided them to an inhospitable area of the Southern Ocean to make it difficult and time consuming for the searchers. And come to mention time – there is another, horrendous mistake been made here.

The absolute maximum flight time left after the final communication from the cockpit till the plane would have run out of fuel was seven hours (the maximum flight time from Kuala Lumpur), minus the one hour flight time taken to the last communication. This leaves six hours absolute maximum; so how did the scientist studying the Inmarsat satellite data say they had a communication with the aeroplanes' engines seven hours after the final communication? Impossible; that is an hour too long.

So what are we to make of these anomalies? The fact that the aeroplane did not have enough fuel to reach where they say it did, and that the jet engines were apparently still communicating with the satellite, when in fact it had probably crashed more than an hour before, and by the information the authorities were giving us, should have been destroyed and lying on the bottom of the Ocean miles deep by then. Is it possible that someone tampered with this data?

Anyway, the Chinese were not fooled by this smoke and mirrors, and obviously did their own calculations just as I have and decided to search much further north, in an area of calmer waters, away from the 'Roaring Forties' that everyone else had been sent to. They searched for weeks to no avail, but hardly altered their search zone, seeming convinced that this is where the plane came down. They were searching in an area where the water had a depth of four thousand five hundred metres at its shallowest. Then out of the blue they detected a signal of the correct frequency, which would indicate they were close to one of the black boxes. Hang on a moment though, this was in fact after the four-week period we were told the batteries in the black box would become exhausted. Then they picked up another signal, then another.

Not one person in a position of authority seemed to say 'wait a minute guys, that is impossible', because I did. The 'pings' given off by these black boxes could only travel a maximum of two thousand metres in water and that would mean that at the depth of water there they would be out of reach and we are expected to believe that they heard it in water way more than least twice that depth. The guy that heard it first was in a rubber dingy with a sonar listening device on what looked like a cheap fishing rod. That's not very James Bond is it? Rubbish.

You, like I, may well believe that to be nonsense. I believe that a 'pinger' locator similar to the one from the missing aeroplane was in fact attached to the outside of an American nuclear submarine, and was being navigated around underneath the Chinese boats so that they would pick the signal up and thus verify the flight went down in that part of the ocean. The Captain of the US nuclear submarine messed up though, he inadvertently allowed the signal to be detected by an Australian ship, also searching with their acoustic microphones, some three hundred miles from the GPS reference point where the Chinese had detected it, and this was only twelve hours later. Again, this was in water four thousand five hundred metres deep. Just a small point. The American Military likes a boast, and the favourite boast of their submarine fleet is that no nuclear submarine of theirs has ever been acoustically detected whilst at sea. That will explain why the Chinese and Australian guys listening to their microphones did not hear any engine noises or any other strange sounds that would have aroused their suspicions. It at least proved there is some merit to the submarine fleets boasting.

So the CIA could have very easily substituted the data in the black boxes and then attached them to a submarine to prove to everyone that the final resting place of the missing aeroplane was in fact the Southern Ocean. Even if the black boxes are never recovered, in fact, if nothing of the plane is ever recovered, then the fact they were detected there would be enough to satisfy most people that this is where the aeroplane came down. However there are the four Emergency Locator Transmitters on the Boeing 777 aeroplane and these would pose a much more difficult problem for the CIA. Let us look at them.

On this variant of the Boeing 777 there are four Emergency Locator Transmitters (ELT), these are designed on more modern aeroplanes to detect when the aeroplane is about to crash, the ELTs do this by being connected to the aeroplanes mainframe computer. Once the aeroplanes' computer senses terrain or water in too close a proximity, by using its flight radar, it would sound the 'Pull up terrain' audio warning. This in turn would arm the ejectors for the ELTs, which would then wait until the main computer sensed they were terminally close to the ground, and then they would fire at about one hundred feet above the surface. This would throw the ELTs away from the crash site and offer them the best chance of surviving and then raising the alarm.

On an older aeroplanes, such as this one however, the ELTs are capable of being deployed in three ways, either manually by the crew before a crash, by the crash impact itself, or by sinking with an aeroplane and as they are positively buoyant, just floating to the surface. This is obviously a haphazard way for the ELTs to be deployed, as there seems to be a significant reliance on luck for them to be able to do the job they were designed for. It is possible that the ELTs did not detach and sunk intact with the aeroplane. They cannot send their signal through water and need to float to work. They are in fact switched on by being submersed. A further almost incredible piece of information is that the Malaysian Airline says it has no record of the servicing of these ELTs throughout their lifespan. Perhaps the batteries had long since become useless and thus rendered the

ELTs useless. Either way, the US Military and the CIA would be able to circumvent the ELTs transmissions anyway. The Island Base at Diego Garcia has, as every American Airbase has, the ability to jam radar signals, and in fact radio signals as well. They could very easily use the AWAC radar aeroplane they have at their disposal do this. It is in fact very old technology and widely used by many militaries.

The fact that none of the four ELTs gave off a signal is further proof that the military may have been involved. Had the plane gone down in the Southern Ocean as we are led to believe – probably having run out of fuel – then I personally think we would have had a satellite pick up the ELT distress signal. It is what they are designed to do remember, survive a crash, float and signal. The other theory is of course that the plane did not crash, but we would have heard something, or found them by now surely.

No ELT distress warning detected.

The satellite company that operates the Inmarsat satellite picking up data from the jet engines more than an hour after it would have run out of fuel.

The Chinese and Australians detecting the black box pings in water, way to deep to ever have been real.

The pings from the black boxes being detected three hundred miles apart in twelve hours.

The Malaysian Prime Minister declaring everyone dead without one piece of evidence he could use to prove it. The pinger locator being put on a boat and actually finally deployed after the four week battery life of the black boxes was up.

The search being sent to the most inhospitable and deepest part of the Southern Ocean, when the plane could never have reached there, in fact it would be lucky to get within fifteen hundred miles of there.

The fact they never used drones to look for the wreckage ... and they are the best piece of equipment they had for that job.

The fact the Americans immediately contradicted the Malaysians when they said that terrorism was not involved. How could they know that?

Not one piece of verifiable wreckage or luggage has ever been found.

The satellite imagery of everything from complete aircraft to huge pieces of the fuselage, and still not one piece was ever seen, let alone recovered.

The lies about the cargo manifest. It actually had hundreds of kilos of lithium batteries on board and they lied about it. If they lie once it is a sure indication they have something to hide.

Two Iranians on board with false passports being declared non-terrorists because one of their mothers says so; you've got to be kidding me.

The plane flying in a manner that every aviation expert, military or civilian agrees makes it look like he is trying to avoid radar. Why did he do this if he intended on flying to the Southern Ocean to commit suicide. He would not care about radar. Why fly an extra four hours to do it anyway?

The fact that the Pilots' own flight simulator was handed over to the Americans. Surely this would never happen unless there was something to hide. The Malaysians' computer guys could easily decipher anything it had hidden in it without any need for American help.

The utter conviction that everyone had in the untried data and people at Inmarsat, and the fact that they have been believed throughout, without question, despite the fact that they said they had data from a jet engine that should have been sunk an hour and ten minutes before they say they got it. They were believed and then very convincing satellite images showed up of large pieces of fuselage almost immediately, and everyone stopped looking anywhere else for the plane.

The fact that the Americans have a defence system that has been in place to globally track aeroplanes that behave in the very way this aeroplane did, and they say they never saw it.

The fact that an aeroplanes cockpit could very easily be taken by terrorists is also frightening, but sadly, very true.

So what is left for the CIA to do with the wreckage of flight MH 370 and the remains of the people that died on that flight? I believe they will dump the aeroplane and the remains of everyone, and the re-programmed black boxes in the Southern Ocean. If they are found, or not, it will make no difference. There will be no reason ever proved for this catastrophe, even if the wreckage is found. The black boxes will offer no solutions. The families will have no closure.

The removal of the debris from Diego Garcia and subsequent repositioning at the Phantom crash site

> will require careful planning, but it is a very straightforward operation.

I believe that some of it may have to be towed behind a ship in large nets – including the bodies of the crew, passengers and hijackers I may add, where it would be very easily cut free by divers, and allowed to sink to the depths. The two on board black boxes would be dropped as well in order to complete the crash site, but they might not risk this. A mystery is probably better for the CIA.

> The CIA are masters of deception. They are very capable of handling this operation, and doing so without leaking any information. They are, however, fallible and the hurried nature of this operation has led to a number of mistakes.
>
> The Military personnel on Diego Garcia would be unaware of this operation, with the exception of the fighter pilots who were sent to intercept. Scrambled fighters are typically sent in twos to allow for some operational cover should anything untoward happen to one of the fighters. Radar personnel would have also witnessed the shooting down incident. Some loadies would perhaps have noticed one of the fighters returning with missing missiles and depleted numbers of canon rounds, but they are well drilled not to ask questions and this could be easily explained away.

Conclusion

So it brings us to the inevitable and perhaps frightening conclusion that the plane must have crashed elsewhere, it's the only summary that fits and that can only mean in my opinion that there is a government sponsored cover up. The appearance of the black box pings in the deep southern ocean without a debris field proves this.

I honestly believe the passengers were murdered almost immediately after the hijack, this is the only explanation for the rapid climb to 45,000ft. The hijacker had subsequently shown great resolve and skill in flying out of the reach of the civilian and military radar, even dropping the plane down to 5,000ft to defeat it, so there must have been a very good reason to climb so high and expose himself to the very radars he was clearly trying to avoid. The silencing of the passengers and in particular crew and flight crew must have been paramount to his plan.

If this was a political hijack then he would have happily allowed them to communicate, as this would raise the profile of his political statement.

If this was someone trying to commit suicide by crashing the plane his first act would be to crash it head first at a dive into the ocean, and this has been done five or six times by pilots before and in each case they have crashed immediately they have complete control of the flight deck, so no need to worry about the passengers or switching off of communications or anything else, why be so complicated?

If he was planning on taking the plane to use as a weapon then why take it earlier than on the day needed and why run the risk of the mission being compromised on the ground?

If this was someone who had simply lost his/her mind then surely this would prove too complicated to achieve. Especially tricking the other flight crew member. He would need to be an exceptional actor.

If this was someone intent on hijack/murder then robbery of dead people and subsequently making his escape by parachuting into a remote dense jungle at night and the huge risks involved in that there would need to be a greater payload he could steal – not enough money – the pilots were earning more than the payoff for a years salary.

Was there perhaps someone on board worth kidnapping and murdering a whole flight to get?

Well there were a number of scientists on board that worked for the American company Freescale Semiconductors. They are developing and producing embedded hardware technologies. There are many countries around the world that would pay big money for their knowledge. The problem is the logistics in lifting them from the plane whilst keeping everyone else quiet, by perhaps murdering the others? It seems crazy and I'm prepared to bet that the technologies they are developing are on the internet already, so hijack for the knowledge held by peoples expertise on board – it's a no for me.

If this was someone intent on hijacking the plane with the intention of flying it to the southern ocean and crashing there in order to commit suicide, with callous disregard for 238 other people on board, why worry about radar? Why care about that? There is nothing to be gained from flying at 5,000ft. Anyone that was so committed to his own demise wouldn't care if radar saw him; what could they do?

The Governments of the USA and Malaysia would have us believe that the plane was hijacked by the captain. They have allowed enough suggestive information to be released into the media to ensure this is the accepted conclusion drawn by most. They would have you believe that the flight MH 370 was then thrown about the sky in order to defeat civilian and military radar, even though the first act was to climb higher and therefore more visible to radar. They would have you believe the pilot, then descended to 5,000ft in order to defeat radar but was intent on killing himself somewhere deep into the southern ocean and would be required to fly the plane for five hours whilst waiting to do so. I do not know if the captain was responsible or even the copilot and it would be unfair to malign their good names without more proof. I have shown the plane could have been taken by other persons on board. I make no assertions as to who was/is guilty. You will need to draw your own conclusions.

Alleged Lies that have been told

The search teams being sent to the South China Sea on the very first day and not to the Malacca Sea. Minister Hussein was both Minister for Defence and Transport so would have had all the radar data from both Malaysian civilian and military sources and these show, by his admission, that the aeroplane crossed the Malaysian Peninsula into the Malacca Sea. He lied to buy time.

The biggest lie is that Americans do not have the capability or the inclination to track aeroplanes that have missed a recognised waypoint, or have switched off the ACARS transponder or general communication link. They would be leaving themselves open to another jihad attack if they did not have this capability. Everyone in the world knows they have satellites that can track incoming missiles, so they already have the satellite hardware, and they would have us believe they have failed to provide extra software to close this obvious hole in their countries defences. That being the case the Russians could simultaneously explode a nuclear weapon over ten or fifteen cities and strategic military targets in America by simply putting them in the hold of an aeroplane and switching the transponder off! They might have lied, because if they admitted having the technology they would need to admit shooting the aeroplane down.

More importantly the American President has been courting the Iranians help in dealing with the rising Islamic State terrorist group operating in Syria and Iraq. I understand he has in fact personally written a letter to the Ayatollah in Iran to ask for help. The disappearance of flight MH 370 – if it was hijacked by two Iranian men – would have immediately curtailed any deals being brokered between the two countries.

Aviation experts from all over the world agreed that flight MH 370 crashed deep into the Southern Ocean. This is incredible; the aeroplane did not have the fuel to make it there if it flew directly there from Kuala Lumpur, never mind the fact it flew north for an hour and thirty-four minutes. This was said to falsely position the crash in a place that the Americans knew the searchers could not mount an effective search in, because of the depth of water and inhospitable sea conditions. Also because it afforded them deep enough water to operate a submarine in, without being compromised. They could also control the search as they had the one piece of equipment that could locate the black boxes, namely the deep-sea 'pinger' locator towed array. I believe they did this to buy themselves enough time to collect the debris from the actual crash site in the waters north of Diego Garcia.

The Malaysian Government have released information through their sources to implicate Captain Shah in the flight disappearance to gain a political victory over the opposition party as Captain Shah was an ardent supporter of the opposition and in fact a quite high profile, vocal supporter and relation to the opposition leader. The Malaysian Government allowed enough information to be released to blacken his name. He remains, in fact, the one person on board that is proven to be innocent in my mind, as it was Copilot Hamid that made the final communication and not Captain Shah. In my opinion this is as close to proof as you can get that he was not involved.

The Iranians were trying to make their way to Europe to seek asylum. This has been a constant nag in my head since it was released that two Iranian men had boarded the aeroplane using false passports. The whole story behind their presence on board stinks. Let us look at it. The first thing that struck me about this story was the route the men were taking to Europe, From Tehran Airport to Kuala Lumpur, here the story muddles. On the first day we were told that the Iranian man had flown in that morning to Kuala Lumpur. This has subsequently been altered to say that one was there a week and the other four days. How is it possible to make that mistake? In a world of computers it just is not possible. The second leg of their journey was on to Beijing – without spending any time in China – from there on to Amsterdam where they would split up and one would fly to a supposed final destination of Frankfurt, Germany where he would seek asylum on presumably political or religious grounds. The other was to continue on to an as yet undisclosed city in Europe. Those of you familiar with the world map will have noticed the ridiculous route these flights take. Tehran is the capital of Iran which is in the Arabian Gulf, in fact directly across the Arabian Gulf from Dubai, a direct flight from Dubai to Frankfurt takes around five hours, so why didn't the two Iranians just fly to Dubai on their own passports as they did to Kuala Lumpur, and then onto Frankfurt from there?

Why would they fly in completely the geographical opposite direction for approximately eight and a half hours, to then board another flight for five and three quarters hours to then fly a further eleven hours back to Amsterdam, and finally from there the short forty-five minute flight to Frankfurt? Going this route they would also need to pass through passport control on their false passports an incredible nine times more, which would undoubtedly have been the most stressful thing for them to do as they were using passports that were registered as stolen, and increase the risk of being caught. Also I cannot believe they would subject themselves to a further three checks at Amsterdam. Surely they would have taken the train. The younger of the two, Pouria Nour Mohammad Mehrdad an eighteen-year-old, and his accomplice Delavar Seyed Mohammadreza who was twenty-nine, arrived in Kuala Lumpur by first reports a few hours before the flight to Beijing, so it was not as though they had flown to Kuala Lumpur to see that brilliant city. The story was similar for Beijing, which could have possibly explained this route somewhat. Now there is some confusion as to when both men arrived, but I prefer to go with the original statement, which confirms they flew in shortly before Flight MH 370 took off, as it is more likely to be true. There is no way a mistake could have been made in finding out when they arrived in Kuala Lumpur, but now further into the investigation the Malaysian Authorities are saying the younger man, Pouria Mehrdad, arrived a week before MH 370 took off.

I am sceptical of information that Governments release as fact, then being changed to suit their stories. The older of the two Delavar Mohammadreza arrived shortly before MH 370 took off, but they have changed that statement to four days. There is no way that this story is true. They had to have flown to Kuala Lumpur for a reason, pure and simple. Maybe they wanted to double their chances of hijack by adding the extra leg of the journey in? It could be that they were concerned that the opportunity to take the plane may not have presented itself on the first leg of their flight. It might be that they did not want to hijack an aeroplane out of Dubai Airport as it is a place many Iranians visit nowadays, and a flight turning back to fly southeast would be picked up immediately by the American Military as they have AWAC radar capable aeroplane overflying the Gulf of Arabia twenty-four hours a day. For sure a hijacked flight out of Dubai to Frankfurt that had its transponder switched off and was heading in the opposite direction towards the Indian Ocean would be intercepted a hundred times out of a hundred. This is the reason I believe they flew to Kuala Lumpur, where they believed they could hijack the aeroplane away from the eyes of the US Military ... they believed wrongly. America saw them and tracked them and they didn't even know. The age difference between the two men is perhaps significant also, one is eighteen and the other is twenty-nine, could it be that one is in charge of the other, like a sergeant to private in the army? Difficult to see where these two could have become friends and been able to discuss the possibility of seeking asylum ... it just seems strange. They were also pretty well funded, the stolen passports would not be cheap and their circumnavigation of the globe with all the flights would be expensive also.

Something else is bothering me, you see Guangzou Airport in Southern China is the relatively new transit hub airport for China, it is in the south of the country and most people that were flying to Amsterdam would transit through here as it is one and a half hours nearer Kuala Lumpur, so why did they book Beijing tickets, could it be that the flight to Guangzou would not have had enough fuel on it to reach Diego Garcia? I can confirm that the Kuala Lumpur to Guangzou flight would have run out of fuel before it reached Diego Garcia and in my opinion that explains why they chose the longer more expensive flight to Beijing, and if anyone can give me another reason for that, I would love to hear it, because it is the only answer I could think of.

We are led to believe that the younger of the two men had a Facebook page and that on it he had admitted to being excited and nervous regarding his trip. Now forgive me if I am being cynical but in a country that is run by Islamic extremists that administer the most oppressive Sharia law there, and that routinely monitors Facebook for inappropriate behaviour and signs of inappropriate behaviour towards the Islamic leaders, are we to believe that a young man would have openly discussed amongst his friends that he was leaving to seek asylum in Europe and would put posts on Facebook regarding this? I am pretty sure he would not. Could he have been nervous because he had decided to join a Jihad mission to attack Americans? The answer to that question, we may never know. One thing is for sure, it is almost impossible to reconcile the route of the journey these men took, without agreeing that there is something extremely strange about them that does not add up.

I was unsure of one thing however, I was unsure if the aeroplane would have enough fuel to reach Diego Garcia if it flew via Maldives. The calculations show it would have had sufficient, but it would be a mighty close thing due the fact the aeroplane was flying lower than at its optimum cruising altitude of 35,000 feet.

The last time an American President visited Malaysia was in 1966, the then President Lyndon Johnson went there to seek closer ties with them as the Vietnamese war had begun and the US were greatly in need of friendly countries in that region. On 25 April fifty-two years later, President Obama should choose to visit Malaysia, so soon after flight MH 370 went missing, on short notice? This was not a trip that had been scheduled months in advance. Should this be written off as a coincidence? Human Rights Watch Asia Advocacy Director John Sifton, has constantly urged the US Government to strengthen their position against human rights violations, and political rights violations in Malaysia. He has even gone so far as to say that personal freedoms are being utterly squeezed by, what is an oppressive regime. He has asked for President Obama to request a personal meeting with the recently jailed opposition leader to try to highlight to the world the lack of civil freedoms and the manipulation by threat of any political opposition. As I said before, the Malaysian Government are perfect examples of absolute power, corrupting absolutely. In an almost unprecedented case, President Obama refused to meet the opposition leader and also refused to mention human rights violations to the Malaysian Prime Minister. This perhaps has the look of one President scratching the back of another Prime Minister in order to keep him sweet. It really is too pathetic for words.

The reason that both of the two Iranians did not show up on any of the international secret service or police data bases that are used to identify terrorists or anyone affiliated to them, is because I believe they were Iranian secret service and they will have no criminal records for the same reason and would have been hand-picked by the Iranians for these reasons. In fact if America or the Malaysians now try to blame the missing flight on the two Iranians on board without being able to tie them to terrorism or the Iranian secret service then public opinion will turn against them for trying to cover up what happened by blaming the hijack on two innocent men. As this book is being written the search for the aeroplane has hit an impasse. The aeroplanes that were searching for wreckage have now been returned to their bases and effectively stood down from the search. Some of the boats have been returned to harbour and the Australian boat that the American military are using as a platform to operate the Bluefin 21 autonomous submarine drone had been in port for two week solid as the bluefin is broken and is waiting on parts for repair. When the boat finally made it back out to the search area the bluefin broke again after two hours in the water and was then further damaged as it was being recovered from the water. This has left a three week period when the search has been halted and no one has been anywhere near to where the suspected Southern/Indian Ocean crash site is. All of this inaction and inept behaviour, I believe, has been manufactured by the Americans. They want to give the outward impression of looking for MH 370, whilst in fact doing everything possible to avoid doing just that.

Now many people will be sceptical if the US military has the ability to track and locate the aeroplane as I have outlined earlier.

I can show that this is indeed the case, very simply. The sad fate of the MH 17 flight that was shot out of the sky over the Ukraine border area has proved that everything I outlined regarding the militaries capabilities to track the aeroplane is factually correct. You see a couple of days after the aeroplane was shot down the US Government released a statement saying they had 'tracked the Russian missile from the moment it was launched until it hit the MH 17 aeroplane.' Now that is very significant. You see they have routinely admitted they have the ability to detect the launch of missiles due to the infrared signature given off at the initiation of launch. Basically this is a multi-satellite system that is designed to look specifically for this heat signature and it covers the entire planet. They have rarely admitted being able to track the missiles and in fact, early on in this terrible saga they even said they had no ability to track missiles or aeroplanes. Yet they released this statement saying they had. Which to me proves they are caught in a lie. It is also very significant that they said 'tracked it until it hit the aircraft'; not tracked it until it exploded. You see if they have tracked it until it hit the aircraft they must be able to see the aircraft. The statements released regarding this kind of thing are scrutinised by many eyes before they are released and the language is always accurate. It is a simple case of careless language showing the truth, hidden in their lie?

I can further show the US government and military are lying by pointing out another undisputable fact. I will outline it below.

During the cold war the US government tasked the US military with keeping track of the submarine force of the USSR (basically Russia). This presented the greatest danger to the USA of any of the USSR weapons as it had the potential ability to covertly approach the shores of the USA and there launch its missiles from close range and thus greatly reduce the missile flight time, thus cutting down America's time to respond. They even potentially had the capability to decapitate the US nuclear arsenal in a pre-emptive nuclear strike. The missiles launched from the Russian subs could hit their targets in as little as seven minutes and therefore was a source of much consternation to the Americans. At its height the Soviets possessed nearly 90 nuclear submarines with an enormous arsenal of hydrogen bombs on board that had the capability of wiping America off of the face of the earth and the USA couldn't build enough attack submarines to keep track of them all. In fact they outnumbered the US submarine force three to one. The Americans countered this threat by building their own submarine launched nuclear missile fleet, the military theory being that if you attack us you can destroy us but we will do the same to you; effectively rendering a nuclear attack from either side as an un-winnable military option. However, the US military felt it only prudent to try and keep track of the submarine fleet of the USSR, as, if they were able to accurately position the submarines around the globe, they would perhaps be able to use this information to work out the strategic thinking of the Russian commanders. Basically if the Soviet submarine fleet all put to see at one time, or if they closed their positions to a point where they could strike at the US mainland or military infrastructure, then that could be seen as a potential first step in a Soviet pre-emptive strike, and the US government and military could take measures to step up their own level of preparedness.

The difficult thing would be how to track the submarines. The US military came up with an ingenious solution. It designed a super sensitive hydrophone, basically an underwater listening device, and then set about positioning these around the world's seas and oceans. This would be referred to as the SOSUS system. It remains the most expensive defensive military project undertaken by the US military, ever. It cost many hundreds of billions of US dollars to design, manufacture, deploy and monitor. It was brilliantly effective. Or rather IS brilliantly effective. You see, so sensitive are these hydrophones that they can pick up a submarine, which are incidentally designed and manufactured to run as quietly as humanly possible, at distances of one thousand kilometres.

In fact to keep track of the submarines movement a sophisticated computer diagnoses the acoustic information gathered from all the sub-surface and on-surface buoys and using a triangulation of information, can pinpoint the position of the submarines to a few metres. These positions are constantly updated. It also has proven to be superbly capable at tracking surface ships. The system is so refined that it can distinguish not only the type of submarine but in fact the individual number of each submarine. That is correct; you did just read that, the system can individually identify the minute differences the nuclear reactors make on these submarines. Now just think about that. I would imagine that nuclear reactors are built to infinitesimally small tolerances. I mean almost indiscernibly small tolerances, they are all built in the same factory and surely the work is of the highest human capability, yet these acoustic microphones can detect the differences, underwater with all the background noise that the ocean creates.

Furthermore they can do this at huge distances. Now the point I am trying to make is that this hyper sensitive system would pick up and identify an aeroplane crashing into the ocean, a fairly noisy event I am sure we would all agree, over a vast number of the hydrophones, and would be able to pin point the position of the crash within a few tens of metres or less and they have not offered one piece of information to this effect. If anyone doubts the veracity of this statement it is a matter of public record that the SOSUS system is there, and it has been used in the past to pinpoint downed Russian submarines, specifically one that exploded underwater – USSR submarine K129 – and was then unsuccessfully attempted to be recovered by the US military in Project AVORIAN.

The microphones that triangulated the position of that submarine were as far away as 3,000 kilometres. Now I agree that an underwater explosion is probably louder than the surface noise made by a crashing aeroplane but I firmly believe that the system would have detected it, and I think I can prove it.

Every so often a large piece of man-made space debris comes crashing back to earth. These range in weight and size but are all significantly smaller and lighter than a Boeing 777. Now thankfully none of these that have fallen to earth have landed on significantly built up areas, and most have crashed into the oceans, where some have been detected by the SOSUS system as they hit the surface, specifically the ROSAT German satellite that made an uncontrolled re-entry in 2011 and crashed into the Indian Ocean. This was a fairly large satellite, however the majority of it burnt up on re-entry and the surviving piece was estimated to be no larger than 500kgs. Regardless of how you word it, if it can detect a piece of metal 500kgs in weight hitting the water, it can detect a 70 tonne aeroplane doing the same.

Onboard the aeroplane were many sealed containers, air tight in fact, bottles in luggage, simple cans of coke, Tupperware, food containers, and obviously the fire proof boxes the lithium batteries were in. The significance of these is very simple. Even if the sonar buoy and hydrophones did not pick up the noise of a seventy tonne aeroplane crashing into the sea, which is inconceivable, they would have definitely picked up the loud popping noise given off as these sealed containers sunk with the aeroplane beyond their crush depth. The noise is a very specific noise that the computers that dissect the SOSUS gathered information are designed to identify. The noise a large airliner makes as it falls to the seabed is quite substantial, this noise is generated by the items on board reaching their maximum crush depth and then succumbing to that pressure in an instant, this causes a cavitating bubble and the collapsing bubble makes a lot of noise, rather like a balloon bursting except in reverse, and it is impossible to believe that such a sensitive array would miss such a loud and obviously man made event.

So where does all this lack of information leave us? Is this just simply the US military and government refusing to release information to try to protect pieces of secret military hardware?

Well I do not think we can accept that excuse. The SOSUS system is so well known that many of the people reading this with no military background will have heard of it, and it has been the subject of a Discovery Channel programme regarding the Operation Avorian attempt to raise K129. The US government and Military have publicly spoken about it; so it is no secret. The ability of the US to track the aeroplane is perhaps a different matter, as they might be trying to keep a lid on that one, however, they could have tracked it to its final destination and then said they heard it on the SOSUS hydrophones and thus released the final resting place of the aeroplane without compromising the secrecy of their tracking capabilities. The fact they have not done this might lend people to suspect they have something to hide.

Some six months after the aeroplane was declared lost a statement was released out of the blue confirming that another aeroplane had in fact contacted flight MH370 over the short-range radio, on the fateful night, after it had changed course and switched its communications off. The statement saying that the pilot of another airliner had hailed MH370 and tried to communicate with the flight crew but had only received a low mumbling in response. Let us deal with this statement.

Firstly I find it absolutely unbelievable that a random pilot would try to communicate with another aeroplane unless there was good reason – say bad weather, or the aeroplane flying in an incorrect corridor, or unless the pilot felt there was generally a good reason. Surely if another aeroplane had communicated with a passenger aeroplane and had only received mumblings as a reply he would raised the alarm; immediately. Secondly, if this had in fact happened on that particular night we would have heard about it within a few very short days, as this was the biggest story throughout the world at that time, and especially as the person trying to communicate with MH370 was a commercial pilot himself.

The chances of another commercial pilot trying to communicate that night with an unknown 777 and then he failing to bring that to the authorities attention is utter nonsense – that could not – and did not happen. If the Malaysian authorities felt it was necessary to keep this information from the public then what was the reason? I can think of none. The pilot of the other aeroplane must have an onboard radar signature to have realised there was another aeroplane nearby as we know the MH370 transponder was switched off or inoperable. This would give us a definite position of the aeroplane and would in fact be the last known and affirmative location. This has never been released. Furthermore, more embarrassingly, we have consistently been told that the communications on board flight MH370 were switched off or inoperable, so how could there have been a communication and mumbling heard? Lies?

The communication on the aeroplane is a simple affair, if someone talks to you on an open microphone you have to open your own microphone to answer. So, if someone was coherent enough to hear, understand and then open a microphone to answer a communication from another aeroplane then surely they would be able to speak or shout a reply, and all this when the communications are said to be switched off. It just does not make sense, and in fact looks like another quickly pieced together untrue statement from the Malaysian Government.

So what does this show us? Firstly it shows that the US Government has known all along where the downed aeroplane was, even before it found its final resting place. Secondly it shows that they had multiple ways of pinpointing the position of the aeroplane in the water. I personally have wracked my brains to think of another reason why the US Government would withhold this information and cannot come up with a realistic answer other than the suggestion that they were somehow involved.

I did however think early on in this disaster that the US was using their knowledge of the aeroplanes whereabouts as a lever on the Malaysian Government to force their hand to take a more aggressive stance with the Chinese in the South China Sea area. Malaysians have one of South East Asia's most modern and capable militaries and it is no secret that the US have been trying to pressurise the nations surrounding China to take a stronger stance against the Chinese to try to curb their ever increasingly aggressive tendencies in that area. Whether the weak political position of the Government in Malaysia made them comply with the Americans demands thereafter I guess we will never know. The surprise visit by President Obama shortly after the flight went missing is perhaps a sign that this was in fact the case.

The fact remains I believe, that whatever the reason the US know exactly where that aeroplane is, where it crashed, and why. They are withholding the evidence for a reason that we cannot definitively say, but it must be very important for them to bury the information in this manner. The saddest fact of all is that the human tragedy has been disregarded by the Governments at the centre of this mystery. The feelings of heartache of the families and friends are seen as secondary to the importance of US interests.

Postscript

As a postscript to this book there is something else that has occurred to me that has a link to this mystery. Two months ago another Malaysian Airlines aeroplane, flight MH 17 was shot down over the Ukrainian airspace on the west side of their border. The international community has accepted that the blame for this tragedy lies at the door of the Russian separatists fighting a civil war in the Ukraine. This would appear to be a terrible coincidence for Malaysian Airlines coming so close after the MH 370 disappearance and many analysts believe it may force the Airline into corporate administration or worse. Whatever the financial outcome the Malaysian Government will probably need to pump large amounts of money into the company to keep it operating or lose an asset that is invaluable at bringing foreign money into the country. Worldwide airports have been shown to generate enormous wealth for the country and cities from where they operate, and a National airline is an intrinsic part of this equation.

I, however, am less convinced that this was a coincidence, or an accident. There are a number of ways the surface to air missile battery could use to identify the

MH 17 flight as a civilian aircraft. The aeroplane had its transponder on and this alone would have been enough to identify the aeroplane to the weapons systems as it has a transponder recogniser as part of its' safety mechanisms. The by-passing of this safety mechanism would take a deliberate action by the weapons controller in the form of a manual override by punching in a key pad code. Similarly the aeroplane was flying at 35,000 feet and on a recognised commercial air traffic corridor, which would also have been known to the weapons operator. Furthermore, the aeroplane had been flying in a fixed direction and had been for hundreds of miles, which military aeroplanes would never do. The aeroplane also had its communications fully established. I believe the Malaysian aeroplane was specifically selected as a collateral target because it was from the Malaysian airline. The separatist soldiers fighting the Ukrainian Government forces in that country have been covertly supported by the Russian President Vladamir Putin, and whilst they deny this in word, they have been shown to have actively supported the separatists with armaments, some special forces, and basic logistics.

The missile battery that shot down MH 17 being an obvious piece of Russian military hardware that the separatists could never have laid their hands on without Russian support. The operating of what is a fairly complex piece of equipment, that takes a lot of training, and it is my contention that the skills to do so would have to have been imported from Russia also. I feel that perhaps the shooting down of the Malaysian aeroplane, Flight MH 17 was retaliation, for the Russians know full well what happened to MH 370, and in a show of callous defiance to America, shot down their own Malaysian aeroplane, in effect telling the American and Malaysian hierarchy, we know what you did. I have no way of proving this but am very suspicious of this incident, and coincidences always bother me.

Lightning Source UK Ltd.
Milton Keynes UK
UKOW04f0950240615

254040UK00001B/10/P